In Search of a Miracle

IN SEARCH OF A MIRACLE

▼

God's Path to Healing

Hugh and Khara Bromiley

Writers Club Press
San Jose New York Lincoln Shanghai

In Search of a Miracle
God's Path to Healing

Writers Club Press
an imprint of iUniverse.com, Inc.

For information address:
iUniverse.com, Inc.
5220 S 16th, Ste. 200
Lincoln, NE 68512
www.iuniverse.com

Credit for Graphic: Nancy Hamilton

ISBN: 0-595-18785-4

Printed in the United States of America

To our good friend the Reverend Al Durrance
who has walked the healing path of Christ
and guided many others along the way.

One day to live

Had I but this one day to live,
One day to love, one day to give,
One day to work and watch and raise
My voice to God in joyous praise,

One day to succor those in need,
Pour healing balm on hearts that bleed,
Or wipe the tears from sorrow's face
And hearten those in sad disgrace–

I'd spend, O God, much time with Thee
That Thou might'st plan my day for me.
Most earnestly I'd seek to know
The way that Thou would'st have me go,
For Thou alone canst see the heart–
Thou knowest man's most inward part.

Alice M. Muir

CONTENTS

▼

FOREWORD

▼

This wonderful book 'In Search of a Miracle—God's Path to Healing' is must reading on the part of all people, whether they are present possessors of an illness or whether they think themselves entirely well. The book is a positive prescription for not only how to get well but how to stay well and how to stay victorious through belief in God's holy healing Word. This is a scriptural book, an excellent book with most interesting testimonies. It is the product of a Christian couple who have walked hand in hand with the healing Savior for many years of their Christian ministry.

William Standish Reed. M.D. Author. Surgery of the Soul
Christian Medical Foundation. Tampa, Florida.

ACKNOWLEDGMENTS

We would like to thank the people who have been an inspiration and a help to us on God's healing path:

Archbishop George Carey; Monsignor Michael Buckley; Doctor Bill Reed; The Reverend Francis MacNutt; The Reverend Al Durrance; Bishop Alex McCullough; The Reverend Rufus Womble; Joanne Peterson; Julabeth Carden; Nancy Bland; Wesleigh Shellman; Meta Moore; Ralph & Ginny Pankoski; Ron & Raylene Poitz; Gene & Vela Rexford; Tom & Maxine Lyttle; Chris & Kathy Forrest; Frances Conner; Susan Ostrem; Cynthia Tynes; Hilda Knowles; Michael Moore.

We are also especially appreciative of Caitlin Taylor Macatee for the gift of joy.

And we are glad to thank the many people who have participated in healing services and conferences with us and who have waited patiently for the arrival of this book.

INTRODUCTION

▼

"Glory to God, whose power, working in us can do infinitely more than we can ask or imagine." (Ephesians 3:20. RSV)

There is an enormous need for healing in this world. Everywhere there are people suffering physically, emotionally or spiritually. Even though some diseases have been conquered in our lifetime others have emerged to take their place as the major threats to health. Both individually and collectively throughout society there is a great deal of stress and distress. The need for healing at this time could hardly be greater.

As the authors, it is our hope that this book will be more than just a book about healing. We hope that it will be a healing book. It is our intention that through reading and reflection you will find your faith in God strengthened and that the power of prayer will be effectively released in your life.

"May God bless you with better health."

We believe prayer and God's miraculous healing are complementary to medical treatment, not a substitute for it. If you are sick you should consult with a licensed physician and follow the directions of your doctor. We encourage you to also incorporate the knowledge given in this book and take advantage of God's healing power.

"Honor the physician with the honor due him, according to your need of him, for the Lord created him: for healing comes from the Most High." (Ecclesiasticus 38:1,2)

CHAPTER ONE

▼

OUR PATH TO THE MIRACULOUS

We would like to begin by sharing with you our journey on God's path to healing.

Hugh and I were in our final year of seminary at Trinity College, in Bristol, England. We had no doubt that God had called us to the ministry. We were not exactly sure where God was leading us. But we were absolutely certain that he was. I (Khara) had been recently diagnosed with a liver disease and the prognosis did not look good. It was hard to believe that God would lead us this far only to let me die of this disease. I was very scared and depressed.

I returned to California to visit one more liver specialist. I will never forget this doctor's visit. There was a microwave oven in the corner of his office. He asked me to excuse him as he went over to the microwave and removed a bag of popcorn. He dumped it into a bowl and remarked how he was addicted to popcorn. He sat down and proceeded to flip through my file. I was extremely nervous. It had been a year since my last test and I had been feeling progressively worse. He told me that my blood clotting factor was virtually non-existent and said that I shouldn't get in a wreck and he laughed. He also suggested I might want to get a medical alert bracelet. Then, between bites of popcorn, he gave me the bad news on my most recent test results. He said that with the degeneration of my liver I had only six months to live, maybe a year at the outside. His face never changed from a stick-on half smile throughout the entire visit. I was shocked at how unconcerned and completely uncaring he was with me. To this day I cannot bear the smell of popcorn. I was on the verge of tears and I went to the ladies rest room, determined not to let this cold doctor see a single tear from me.

I composed myself in the ladies room and washed my face. As I came back out into the hallway a sweet looking nurse stood there with my file in hand and asked me to follow her to the front desk, where I was promptly presented with a bill for $285.00. I stood looking at it for a second and then I looked at her and heard myself saying "I don't pay for bad news served up so cold and anyway dead people don't have to pay!" I put down the bill and walked out of the office leaving one stunned nurse and a few startled patients. I never did receive another bill from this doctor's office!

I subsequently went to another doctor, looking for another opinion and hoping against hope to hear something more encouraging. Although this doctor was much more caring in his manner, the verdict was still basically the same, that I would be unlikely to live longer than two years. Well, at least two years sounded better than one! Soon a third doctor offered the same dire prognosis. All the doctors were in agreement that there was no cure. Anyway by now we knew very clearly that it was time for us to put our trust and faith in God. In truth there really wasn't any alternative. We went back to the college, taking one day at a time. We quickly learned to live in the present and to value each day and each other as a gift from God.

As was our custom in the theological college, we would meet with fellow students for tea and prayer. We would often share information and books. Initially I was extremely reluctant to tell anybody about my illness. But Hugh felt strongly that it was important for me to have the prayers and support of others. One of our friends, who was from Ireland, offered to loan me a book on healing, "His Healing Touch" written by an Irish Catholic priest, Monsignor Michael Buckley. As we read this book we began to feel some encouragement for the first time since the diagnosis. It also led us to want to seek out a Christian healing service. That did not seem to be as easy to do as we at first assumed it would be.

A few weeks after I returned the book to my friend, he said to me, "by the way, Monsignor Michael Buckley will be holding a two day healing conference with services in London in a couple of weeks." I could hardly believe this quick answer to our prayers. Well, we have all heard the saying that 'God works in mysterious ways' and he surely did. We had to make some changes in our schedule so that we could be in London for the two days.

Having gone to a Baptist Church as a young girl, I found it hard to imagine what a Catholic healing service would be like. I felt a strange mixture of curiosity, hope and apprehension. We arrived early on the Friday evening at a large Catholic Cathedral. Crowds of people were lined up at both doors. All types of people, many of whom looked seriously ill, some of them with prayers on their lips and a rosary in their hands, were waiting to get in, waiting for the healing touch of God. We were amazed at the number of people there. When we filed into the cathedral, we could see that it held about two thousand people. We wondered if it was going to be big enough for the crowd that was growing outside. We were ushered over to seats on the right side of the cathedral directly behind a large marble pillar. I was disappointed that I could not see the altar or the pulpit better from where we were sitting. Although I was a bit nervous, I was also excited and I felt a sense of expectancy.

We all stood as three priests processed to the altar. There was no doubt in my mind which one was Monsignor Michael Buckley. He was a tall, slender man with thick, silver-gray hair. His eyes were the intense bluish color of cornflowers and they had a special light in them. On top of all this, he had that wonderful Irish lilt to his voice. Not even a Hollywood director could have put together this place, the priest and the people in the way that God did to set the scene for miracles. We sang songs of praise to God. Monsignor Buckley thanked God for all the wonderful healing that he had seen God bring about. He told us to look around at the other people in the pews and reminded us of the necessity of getting our minds off our own illnesses and concerns, and to pray for others. Later, when the collection plates were passed, he did something I had never seen before or since in a church! He said, "If you have money please give as generously as you can. If you have no money and you are in need, please take some money to meet your need."

Monsignor Buckley went on to explain how the Holy Spirit worked with him. He said that he would walk down the aisles of the cathedral until the Holy Spirit told him to stop and go over to a particular person and lay hands on them and pray and anoint them with oil. Having said that, he and the two other priests began to walk down the aisles to pray for and bless the people. If the person he felt led to pray for was far down the aisle, he would call them out to the aisle, or sometimes he would just lean over, reaching out an outstretched hand toward the person. All this took a while. There was a lot of intense emotion in the air and many people were crying. The sound of sobbing mingled with the sound of prayers and resounded through the cathedral. But I began to feel disappointed and deprived because he had not come over to pray for me. We were sitting so far from the center aisle and now he seemed to be returning to the altar. Then quite suddenly he walked down our side aisle and he pushed past my husband, trying to reach me. For a moment he held my head in his hand and prayed for me in words that I cannot remember, except that he assured me that God would make me alright. I felt intense heat starting in my head and spreading down through my body. I started to feel my anxiety fade. For the first time since the onset of the disease a sense of peace came over me. There was no doubt in my mind that I was receiving a healing touch from God. Monsignor Buckley moved on and continued to pray for people. As the congregation sang, Hugh and I held hands and through our tears we thanked God.

A woman and a young girl suddenly pushed towards a microphone near the altar. From the look on the face of one of the assisting priests this was clearly not part of the program. He stood up but Monsignor Buckley motioned him to sit back down. The woman started to tell how ten years before, after being told that her baby had no hope of surviving, she had brought her baby home from the hospital to die. As a last desperate hope she had bundled her up and had brought her to a healing service at the cathedral, hoping that Monsignor Buckley would pray for her. But with so many people there it did not happen and she left the church bitterly disappointed. Completely distraught and in tears, she resigned herself to the inevitable. The next morning she awoke abruptly, shocked that she had fallen asleep. She looked over, half expecting her baby to be dead and to her delight she saw a smiling and contented looking baby.

Then she said, "I want you to know that you don't have to get the touch directly from Monsignor Buckley, or any one special, in order for God to heal you here." She put her arm around her daughter, now ten years old and thanked God for her healing and thanked Monsignor Buckley for his faith in making these healing services available. There was not a dry eye in the cathedral.

At the end of the second day, standing at the front of the cathedral, Monsignor Buckley said that God had just told him that there were two people there, who he should anoint for a healing ministry. He looked around for a moment and did not seem to find who he was looking for. Nobody went forward. Then he spoke again, this time louder and more insistently, and he pointed and said, "back there by that pillar." My husband, Hugh, said, "Come on, he means us," and he tugged on my sleeve. I said "No, he doesn't. I'm not going up there!" There was a short silent pause and at that moment an assisting priest started walking towards us and motioned us to come forward. We went up to the front of the cathedral.

Monsignor Buckley said that God had a healing ministry for us and that he was to anoint us now for that ministry. He told us to hold out our hands with our palms up. He prayed for us and made the sign of the cross with blessed oil in our hands. We both felt the presence of the Holy Spirit and we trembled.

We watched God heal many people in those two days and he changed our lives for ever. It has been fifteen years since I was told that I had only two years to live. We came looking for a miracle for ourselves. God gave us much more than we asked for. He not only gave us our miracle, he also set us on the path of the healing ministry.

CHAPTER TWO

▼

PROOF POSITIVE

Your healing begins with a partnership—God and you. Your job in this partnership is to cooperate with God's divine plan. This strong sense of partnership plays a key role in recovery. God provides the healing. Your part is to be responsive and receptive to the healing that God provides.

Over the years there has been increasing evidence and documentation of people who have been diagnosed with incurable illnesses suddenly recovering. At times these recoveries stun the medical community, invoking terms such as 'remission', 'inexplicable', 'fluke of nature', or even 'miracle'. Did God heal them? As an Anglican priest called to the healing ministry, it has been my privilege to observe a significant number of physical healings that indeed do defy all expectations and at times contradict the prognoses of the medical community. Even more numerous are the many instances of spiritual or emotional healing that also have a beneficial and dramatic impact on a person's overall health. There can be no doubt that God's healing love and power can dramatically change your health and your life.

Recently there has been a growing number of physicians and researchers who have confirmed in scientific terms the truth about the magnificent power of faith and healing prayer. There have been hundreds of studies done in the last three decades in the USA and in Europe that indicate the therapeutic benefits of prayer. Prayer has been shown to be more than just a placebo.

In December 2000 the Wall Street Journal published an article entitled 'The Prayer Cure'. The subheading read, **"Faith healing has gone mainstream, as more churches and synagogues embrace the idea that worship can fight disease."**

In one controlled study groups of people prayed for intensive care patients, having been given only their names and locations. Hospital monitors recorded significant improvements in bodily functions. A double-blind study undertaken at a coronary care unit at San Francisco General Hospital showed that patients who were prayed for did significantly better than those who were not.

In a six month study at California Pacific Medical Center in San Francisco, AIDS patients were prayed for by people from around the world who believe in the healing power of prayer. The patients had fewer visits to their doctors and were hospitalized less often than another group of AIDS patients who were not prayed for.

Studies by Dr. Koenig of Duke University and Dr. Larson of the National Institute of Healthcare Research, have shown that people who attend church regularly have better immune responses and fewer instances of high blood pressure. What's more they live longer than people who don't attend.

Several physicians, whose work has been published, have been courageous in reporting on the positive effects of faith and prayer. Dr. Andrew Weil wrote: **"A considerable body of research data supports the beneficial effects of prayer on health."**

D. B. Larson MD has collated extensive research on the relationship between health and faith for the National Institute for Healthcare research. Dr. Larson has written: "**When studied with measures designed to assess the depth of a person's faith, such as frequency of worship service attendance, of prayer and scripture reading, or of questions raised about one's relationship with God, religious commitment is associated with clinical benefits.**" The Forgotten Factor in Physical and Mental Health: What does the research show? Drs. D.B. and S. Larson.

Dr. Larry Dossey has written: "**After sitting on the sidelines for most of the 20th century, prayer is moving toward center stage in modern medicine. Doctors are taking prayer not just into their offices, clinics and hospitals, but into experimental laboratories as well. Medical journals are more willing than ever to publish studies on the healing effects of prayer and faith.**" Prayer is good medicine. Larry Dossey MD.

Dr. William Standish Reed has written in his book, The Surgery of the Soul: "**The Gospel message is a healing message, and not only are doctors and nurses in need of its possession in their own lives, but man in general, in the desperate hour in which we live in the world today, needs the healing Gospel of Jesus as in no other time.**" Surgery of the Soul. **William Standish Reed MD.**

In 1995 the Journal of the American Medical Association printed an article entitled, '**Should physicians prescribe prayer for health?**' In that article they referred to evidence that prayer is positively linked to health improvements. What faithful believers have known for a long time is being increasingly confirmed by the scientific community. Sick people who are prayed for recover faster. They require less medication and suffer less side effects than those who are not prayed for. Moreover people who are prayed for also generally sustain a much better attitude during treatment. We all intuitively know the valuable role of a person's attitude in healing. Increasingly that role is acknowledged by people in the healing professions.

"**Medical Research is discovering that high determination and purpose can actually enhance the working of the immune system.**" Head First. Norman Cousins

This book is intended to be a guide for people who seek God's healing path. Our aim is to ensure that we are not deprived of the health, well-being and wholeness that God intends for people.

"Although the world is full of suffering, it is also full of the overcoming of it." Helen Keller

The possibility of a miraculous healing can be more than just wishful thinking. But it requires something from us. It is time for us to change, to adjust our thoughts and attitudes and open ourselves to the possibility of healing miracles. We need to encourage faith and come to expect the healing miracles of God in our life. We all need guidance to experience a sense of oneness with God, so that we can be transformed through faith. As we begin to change inwardly, we can accept and receive the healing power of the living Christ.

"Medical Ethics have become mere rules of conduct between doctors and their patients—cold, lifeless, impersonal! Jesus Christ gives to medical ethics their true place, taking into consideration the eternal spirit and man's relationship to God." Surgery of the Soul. Dr. William Standish Reed

CHAPTER THREE

▼

HEALING THE WHOLE PERSON

God is interested in the healing of the whole person. The word 'holistic' has been in use for many years now. In simple terms, it means treating the whole person, not just the symptoms they display. Healing cannot be compartmentalized into physical or mental or emotional or spiritual segments. A person is an integrated, spiritual, psychosomatic whole, not a collection of parts. This understanding of a person 'as a whole', far from being a modern development is consistent with the time-honored biblical understanding of man.

Dr. Paul Tournier in his book 'The whole person in a broken world' makes reference to this unity of a person spiritually, physically and mentally. He wrote: **"Only God who created man as body, soul and spirit can effect this harmonious synthesis in us and society."**

God's love and God's healing are available to all people. Healing is not the unique possession nor the prescriptive right of any one religious denomination. God is God and he can never be dictated to by any group. God's divine love encompasses all people.

Divine healing is more than just getting better. It is being restored to wholeness. Jesus Christ, who is also referred to as the Great Physician, is described as coming to earth to give knowledge of salvation to his people. The biblical word that is translated as 'salvation' can also be translated as 'healing' or 'wholeness'. In other words, God intends for his people to be made whole. The Christ came to bring healing to our spirits and our minds and our bodies.

Jesus referred to his healings as his 'works'. We think of them as miracles. A miracle is defined as being: 'something to wonder at.' It is also described as 'an act of power.' Every healing is a demonstration of the divine power and has an element of the miraculous to it. As E.W.Kenyon wrote in his book, The wonderful name of Jesus: **"Man was brought into being by a miracle working God and man will ever yearn to work miracles."**

We welcome you to an exploration of the miraculous.

CHAPTER FOUR

▼

WHY? WHY? WHY? QUESTIONS AND ANSWERS

As we speak at Healing Conferences around the world we find that there are certain questions which are frequently asked about the healing work of Christ. Often we find that these questions are so dominant in a person's mind, that until their question is resolved they are not able to be open to God's healing. We would like to address these questions up front. The responses provided in this chapter are not intended to be full answers to all the questions, but a brief and clear indication of what we understand God has said on the subject. These points will be explored more fully in following chapters.

1) Are spiritual healings instantaneous?

Healing can indeed occur instantaneously and it is absolutely wonderful when you witness that occurring. However it may occur gradually or over a long period of time. What is important is that you don't give up praying for God's healing love and power.

"Never, never, never give up." Sir Winston Churchill

Do not be discouraged if at first you don't see any apparent physical improvement. Turn to the Lord and to what he has to say: "**He gives strength to the weary and increases the power of the weak. Even youths grow tired and weary, and young men stumble and fall; but those who hope in the Lord will renew their strength. They will soar on wings like eagles; they will run and not grow weary, they will walk and not be faint.**" (Isaiah 40:29-31)

2) Why are some people healed and others are not?

There is no quick or easy answer to this question. We could just respond that we don't know. We certainly don't know all the answers and there are situations that can probably never be explained. However, there are some factors that do make a difference and increase the likelihood of receiving healing. One of the critically important factors is coming to a clear and strong belief that it is God's will for you to be healed. Many other factors that contribute to a person being receptive to divine healing are explored throughout the book.

3) Does healing prayer work from a distance?

Yes, absolutely. Healing prayer does work from a distance. Thousands upon thousands of people have testified to the power of prayer for someone in a different location. Clinical trials have also successfully demonstrated the power of healing from a distance. In a controlled study, groups of people prayed for intensive care patients, having been given only the names and locations. Hospital monitors recorded significant improvements in several bodily functions. However, many people feel that healing prayer is more effective when they are actually present with the person. It cannot be overemphasized that there is tremendous benefit when you combine a caring human touch with prayer.

4) If there is a God, why does he allow evil and sickness in the world?

This is the most frequently asked question. It is important to understand that God created us with free will. If he were to intervene and radically remove all sickness and evil in the world, he would not be taking into account the free will that he gave us. Instead he would be treating us like robots. He would be going against our nature, ignoring our collective choices as the human race, and disregarding the consequences of those collective choices. God wants us to freely make the right choices regarding our life and our health, our beliefs and our behavior. God wants us to receive his healing blessings. God wants us to genuinely desire to live according to his will, but he will not impose his will on us. Please see the chapter on God's will for further explanation.

5) Do I have to be a Christian or be a religious person to be healed?

Quite often people only come to know God when all other alternatives are exhausted and there is nowhere else to turn. Many people become committed Christians after turning to God and experiencing his healing power. God can and does heal anyone. Being a Christian is not necessarily a prerequisite for divine healing. We have had people come to our healing services who were not Christians, who benefited and were healed through his healing love and power. The word religion literally means to 'bind back' to our source, who is God. So when God heals, he is binding us back to him through his love and his life-giving power. However we think that there is another extremely important factor to bear in mind if we want to continue to experience wholeness and spiritual well-being. That factor is showing gratitude and obedience to God. When you think about it, would it not be infinitely better to come to know God first and to already be in relationship with him? How much better would it be to bring our needs and the needs of those we love to God who we already know personally.

6) Is Satan real, and does he send sickness and death to people?

It is very clear that Jesus perceived Satan as being real and as being his adversary. Over the ages faithful Christians have been similarly convinced of the reality of Satan. Satan has continually tried to keep people separated from God and from his love and his power. The Bible teaches that there is a negative spiritual component to illness that Satan has brought into the world. The important thing to keep in mind here is that the power of God is infinitely stronger than the power of Satan.

7) How do I know if I have a gift of healing through prayer?

Put it to the test. Try it and see. Do people have a positive response when you pray for them? The only way to discover this is to undertake a systematic and faithful practice of praying for people in need. It is not enough to try it once or twice and then quit. Our experience has been that the more you pray faithfully for people, the more you see people being healed in response to prayer. This of course builds your faith in prayer and so a beneficent circle has begun, which continues as faithful prayer becomes a more important aspect of your life.

8) Why do people seek out spiritual approaches to healing that are not Christian?

When people experience a need or have a spiritual hunger, but feel, rightly or wrongly, that the Church has not met their need, they may turn to other approaches. It is the responsibility of the Church to be sure that people are presented with the actual experience of the healing living God, not just a diluted dose of religion. People need to get the word out and let others know that God is the source of healing, by telling them of their own experiences of his healing power.

CHAPTER FIVE

▼

GOD ON LINE:\\MOSTHOLYGOD.COM

In recent years the benefits of prayer have become a hot topic for newspaper and magazine articles and talk shows. Prayer has always been a practice of believers and seekers throughout the ages. So, what is it? Why do we do it? How do we do it? Does it work?

God calls us to prayer

"Be joyful always; pray continually; give thanks in all circumstances, for this is God's will for you in Christ Jesus." 1 Thessalonians 5:11-18

The call to prayer clearly and unmistakably shows that God is interested in our lives. In making prayer available to us, he has given us the perfect way to communicate with him. Prayer is like life-giving breath to a believer. Prayer is a practical blessing from God the Father because he loves his children.

In his letter to the Philippians, Paul said: "In everything, by prayer and petition, with thanksgiving, let your requests be known to God." (Philippians 4:6). Every aspect of our lives, great or small, secret or public, sad or happy, can and indeed should be brought before God in prayer. Physical, mental and spiritual health, personal issues, domestic, social, national and worldwide issues all fall within the realm of prayer. We need to let God know through prayer what is going on with our lives. It is not as if he doesn't already know, but he wants us to talk to him about it, bringing it before him in prayer. People have a natural instinct for prayer. We each have an innate desire and ability to talk with our Creator, an instinct that God has placed in every one of us. Prayer is a significant part of being human.

Prayer is deeply comforting. Prayer is extremely powerful. It is true self-expression. Prayer is intimacy with God. It connects us to our Father. Prayer is our responsibility to ourselves as well as to God. In prayer we can share our confidences, withholding nothing from our Father. We can share all our concerns and requests, assured that this outpouring of our heart is heard by God.

Intercessory prayer

A man who was a faithful member of our church and active in our Order of St.Luke healing ministry asked for prayer for his cousin Helen, who lived over a thousand miles away in Missouri. Helen was a young woman who had a malignant tumor on the bone of her right leg. Her cousin was very anxious about her condition and came forward at our weekly healing service to ask for prayer. We laid hands on him and together we prayed for Helen. Her name was also put on the prayer list, which meant that some people prayed for her daily. The next report was that she was scheduled for radical surgery, the amputation of her leg, in one week's time. In spite of this drastic measure she was in very good spirits.

On the three hour drive to the hospital, Helen was recounting to her husband all about her cousin's church in California that was praying for her. She told him how her cousin, who she had not seen in years, was really excited about the miracles he had seen through this healing service. She said that he believed healing prayers would work for her. As she was telling her husband about these people who she had never met, who were praying for her, she began to feel heat in her right leg. She became warm all over and her leg got hotter and hotter. She heard a voice in her head tell her plainly and clearly that she was healed. Incredibly excited, she told her husband, "I'm healed. I know it. I can feel it!" Her husband didn't want to discourage her or dampen her excitement, but equally he didn't want her to delude herself. She told him to turn around and go home and that she did not need any surgery. The pain was gone and so was her fear. He convinced her that they really must finish the trip to the hospital and at least have her leg x-rayed again.

When they got to the hospital Helen and her husband insisted on having another x-ray before the scheduled surgery. To their delight the x-ray confirmed what she already knew inside herself to be true. The tumor was gone and the bone was healed. The doctor told them that in all his years as a physician he had never seen a tumor just disappear like that.

How do we pray?

Prayer is a conversation with God. When we pray it is good for us to invite God to be present with us, to welcome him and to ask him to help us to be aware of his presence. The act of praying is in itself an expression of our confidence that God is now present with us. We can pray silently and we can pray out loud. Prayer can be long and involved or short and direct. Prayer can be standing up, on our knees, sitting down or lying down. We can pray alone or we can pray with someone else. We can pray in small groups or large groups. However we choose to pray our prayers should above all be honest and heartfelt.

When we pray our aim should not be to change God's mind, trying to get him to see things our way. "**For my thoughts are not your thoughts, neither are your ways my ways," declares the Lord.'** (Isaiah 55:8). It is far more valuable to ask God to change us and help us to see things **his** way.

"**Prayer is...talking with God and telling him you love him, conversing with God about all the things that are important in life, both large and small, and being assured that He is listening.**" C. Neil Strait.

How much should we pray?

"Prayer as talking and listening needs to be an important element in our daily walk with God. Don't skimp on it, because the experience of great Christians has been that without it we cannot grow into Christian maturity." I believe. Archbishop George Carey

God says we are to pray without ceasing. With our busy lives this would be hard to imagine. But integrating prayer into each day requires perseverance and persistence. You have to make time for conversations with your heavenly Father. In that sense it is similar to calling your best friend at the same time every day. If you think it is worth it you find the time or make the time. If we undertake any activity whether it is sports or a computer skills class, we don't realistically expect to realize any benefit unless we are regular and consistent in our practice. Although prayer is in a different category from anything else in life, it is nonetheless true that we will more fully realize the benefits of prayer when we apply ourselves. Praying regularly is in itself an expression of our faith.

God may heal a person immediately; he may heal gradually. He may heal someone after prolonged and persistent prayer by hundreds of people; he may heal after just one prayer by only one person. He may heal through the use of medical procedures; he may heal without the use of medical procedures.

"In reliance on the Holy Spirit you will find many of your physical and mental ailments will disappear along with many of your worries, inner conflicts and tensions." Peace with God. Reverend Doctor Billy Graham

Why do we pray?

"Good morning, God. I love you! What are you up to today? I want to be part of it." Norman Grubb

We pray because God asks us to. He wants us to be in touch with him, just as any parent wants their children to be in touch with them. We also pray because we realize that we are not able to handle all our problems, our diseases, our addictions and our temptations by ourselves, using only our will power. If we could manage entirely by ourselves we would already have proved that. But, sooner or later, most of us come to the realization that we need help. In those moments where do we turn? Who do we turn to? Just the opportunity of talking directly with God is a truly awesome and extraordinary privilege. It is here we start to realize the enormous power of prayer. The entire basis of Christian Healing is prayer, calling upon God in the name of his Son Jesus Christ. Take your concerns to God. By taking our concerns to him, we show our absolute respect and our love for him. Every relationship benefits from good two-way communication. Prayer will take you into a right relationship with God the Father.

Does prayer work?

"Whatever you ask for in prayer, believe that you have received it and it will be yours." Words of Jesus (Mark 11:24)

Does prayer work? Jesus says yes. Interestingly, as you can see, a growing segment of the medical community now agrees. Christians have known the power of prayer for two thousand years. Although people generally want proof, faith does not require proof for it to be validated. Prayer can change the strongest emotions. Prayer can curb the most excessive appetites and compulsive obsessions of the human psyche. Prayer can fill us with a personal knowledge of God's desires and plans for our destiny. "And we know that in all things God works for the good of those who love him, who have been called according to his purpose." (Romans 8:28) Prayer makes us open and receptive to God's love and his generous blessings.

"Prayer feeds the soul. As blood feeds the body, prayer is to the soul. It brings you closer to God." A simple Path. Mother Teresa

Parallel Track

Christian healing through prayer is not antagonistic to the practice of modern medicine. Far from it, prayer and medicine complement each other. We do not suggest using prayer instead of medical treatment but as a parallel track to it. Remember that recent studies have confirmed what faithful believers have known for a long time. People who are prayed for do recover faster, require less medication and suffer far less side effects than those who are not prayed for. Moreover people who are prayed for generally sustain a much better attitude during treatment. The role of attitude in healing is increasingly acknowledged by people in the medical professions.

Sometimes we forget to pray for what is most obvious. We should pray about our medical diagnosis and treatment, to pray for God's guidance for our doctors and nurses and other health care practitioners. Many people will offer a prayer of thanksgiving and ask for God's blessing before eating their meals. Doesn't it seem like a good idea to ask God to bless our treatments and medications before we, or someone we are concerned about, use them?

"The world may doubt the power of prayer, but the saints know better." Anonymous

A story about centered prayer

A friend of ours, Jeanne, was undergoing chemotherapy. She was experiencing extremely severe side-effects, including nausea, hair loss and intense pain. Then she started taking a moment to center herself in prayer. She would ask God to direct the chemotherapy treatment to the cancer cells only. She visualized God's Spirit directing the treatment where it was needed and pictured the cancer cells being destroyed. After she started integrating this prayer into her sessions the side effects which had been causing her so much suffering were almost completely eliminated.

"Is any one of you sick? He should call the elders of the church to pray over him and anoint him with oil in the name of the Lord. And the prayer offered in faith will make the sick person well; the Lord will raise him up." (James 5:14,15)

Why is prayer so important?

You may be wondering by now, if prayer is so good and so natural and can heal, why doesn't everyone pray? We wonder the same thing. Perhaps one reason people do not turn to prayer lies in their personal difficulty in reconciling the message of God's love with the everyday problems, sorrows and pains of this life. For whatever personal reason, people have abandoned the practice of faithful prayer and have lost their connection to God the Father. Tragically many people cannot even see the value of prayer.

We must remember that if we stop praying, we inevitably lose the comfort that prayer gives us. God has spoken to us about prayer repeatedly throughout the Bible. He wants us to pray. When we pray according to the will of God, we are praying in the same way that Jesus himself prayed. There is no force on earth that is any stronger. The integrity of God backs up our prayers and his power is fully available to us.

"He who fails to pray does not cheat God. He cheats himself." George Faeling

When we neglect prayer, we close off the direct line between our soul and the living God. We stifle our spiritual expression and choke our lifeline. One of the many remarkable things about Mother Teresa was how tirelessly she worked in terrible conditions right up to the end of her life. She used to say, **"Without prayer I could not work for even half an hour. I get my strength from God through prayer."** What a wonderful gift God has arranged for us that his compassion and power are waiting on the other end of prayer.

"Without constant prayer you never can know the inner peace that God wants to give you. Your prayers may falter at first. You may be awkward and inarticulate. But the Holy Spirit who lives within you will help you and teach you." Peace with God. Billy Graham.

God's Rx:

Pray anywhere, anytime. Pray in your own words.

Have a heart to heart conversation with God and resolve to get into a regular prayerful relationship with him.

CHAPTER SIX

▼

ROADBLOCKS ON THE ROAD TO HEALING

"Enter here the pharmacy of the soul." Engraving over St. Gall Monastery Library

There are many obstacles to healing. Some of them are external, but a lot of them are internal. It is hard for us to admit that we are self-centered rather than God-centered. It is easy to be cynical about Christian healing, especially because it seems to get a surprising amount of negative press. It is our desire to see the ministry of healing restored into the positive light that it so clearly deserves.

We may despair of ever being healed. Many people wonder whether disease and natural disasters are the will of God, or a sign that he doesn't care, or perhaps that he doesn't even exist. Our minds tell us that this illness must be a punishment that we deserve. We may find ourselves feeling jealous when we hear of other people's healing stories. We may find ourselves asking questions of God, such as, 'how come they can smoke and drink and eat whatever they want and I don't, but I'm the one sick? Why me?'

Resentment of other people, self pity and being angry at God are all obstacles to healing. These are just some of the negative thoughts that get in the way of our receiving the Lord's healing.

Do you recognize any of the following thoughts?:

'Why shouldn't I get my healing my way? Why do I need other people to pray for me? Why should I go to a healing service? I don't buy all that laying on of hands stuff! Why should I read the Bible? I can't see that Christian healing could have anything to do with medicine or doctors. I don't have time to eat healthily. I can't stop smoking. I can't quit drinking. I can't forgive…' The list goes on.

"Obstacles are those frightening things you see when you take your eyes off the goal." Anonymous.

God's Rx:

Pray: "Oh God help me to get out of my own way." Reflect on what negative thoughts you have that could be roadblocks to healing. Bring them to God and ask him to help you let go of them.

*   *   *

Think about it

Although the life-giving power of healing comes from God, a person still has an active role to play in their healing. There are certain things that any of us can do that are helpful to the healing process. There are other things that we should cut out of our life because they are clearly harmful.

"If any of you lacks wisdom, he should ask God, who gives generously to all without finding fault, and it will be given to him. But when he asks he must believe and not doubt, because he who doubts is like a wave of the sea, blown and tossed by the wind." (James 1:5,6)

Do you know that when it comes to health, God challenges us to use our minds and he offers us a gift of wisdom to help us? He wants us to use our common sense while bringing balance to our lives. He wants us to take ordinary care of our mental and spiritual health as well as our physical health. In so doing, we will have less need for those extraordinary measures of healing.

When we step into the realm of God's miraculous power we cannot hang on to the old attitudes, the negative thinking, the anxieties and the doubts that have pervaded our minds with unbelief. In our pride and with our constant demand for proof, we have not been willing to humble ourselves before God, and make that essential all out expression of faith. Is it wise to walk in to the Great Physician's (God's) office, looking to him as the last hope? Wouldn't it make more sense to look at God as our first hope?

God offers us the absolute best in preventive medicine. Trying to get healing from medications only without also seeking spiritual help is an age old problem that is referred to back in Old Testament times. "**Though his disease was severe, even in his illness he did not seek help from the Lord, but only from physicians.**" (**2 Chronicles 16:12**). Dr. William Standish Reed has criticized the separation of spiritual healing from physical treatment: "**Medicine today is a natural medicine practiced by men who have basically ignored the spiritual aspect, not only of their patients but also of themselves.**" **Surgery of the Soul. Dr. W. S. Reed**

God's Rx:

It is time to integrate prayer with the best available treatments.

           *   *   *

"Do you want to get well?" (NIV) or "Wilt thou be made whole?" (KJV)

Jesus had just learned that a man he met had been an invalid for thirty-eight years. He asked him, "**Do you want to get well?**" (**John 5:6**). Since we know Jesus was compassionate why did he ask this question? It seems at first like a strange question. Of course a sick person wants to get well! Perhaps, perhaps not. Did Jesus doubt this person's willingness to be open to God's way? Did he doubt this person's desire to be healed? Evidently he did. Did this doubt come from his seeing that this man had surrendered to his illness? It is an important question to consider, whether a person's will to get well might in fact be a key issue regarding their recovery.

We need to ask ourselves candidly whether, unconsciously, we receive some benefit from being sick. This may be a hidden benefit, like getting that extra attention because we have felt unloved by the people closest to us. Many people find that because of their condition, their loved ones have been more attentive and have visited and called them more frequently than before their illness occurred. They don't want to return to the way things used to be before they got sick, when their loved ones never came to see them. We have heard people say, "I guess I'll have to die before anyone will believe that I am really sick. Only then will they know how seriously ill I was all along. Then they'll be sorry!" We have even heard people admit, "my doctor is the only person who really seems to care about me. If I recover I won't be able to see the one person who cares." The fact that this is extremely poor logic is beside the point. The point is that if you like getting extra attention out of being sick, you may not yet be willing to let go of your illness and be freed from your suffering.

Letting go

A young mother who was in what can only be called an abusive relationship had been sick for the entire fifteen years of her marriage. Her life was spent in anxiety waiting for the next group of blood tests or the next MRI with the ever-present fear that this time it was going to turn out to be cancer. She had recently been diagnosed as having pre-cancerous uterine cells and the frequency of her tests had been increased to monthly. With this added stress came the diagnosis of a stomach ulcer. She had started to unravel. As a last resort she begun attending our Wednesday healing service. On the second Wednesday, as she knelt at the altar rail and waited for her turn to be prayed for she started to cry. As I anointed her with oil she suddenly dropped down to the floor. When the prayer time was finished she got to her feet and a little shaken she left the church.

The next week she returned to the healing service a different woman. She told us all that she knew that God had healed her. She described how she had experienced a heat that started at the top of her head and flooded down to her feet. She told us that she had slept well every night of the week without using any sleeping pills. Two weeks later she told us that the latest round of tests had revealed that she was well. Her doctor said that if he himself had not previously examined her he would not have believed that she ever had any of her reported health problems. Within less than a month she had come off all her medications. In the weeks that followed we watched an outer and inner change unfold in her health and her spirit. She is not only well physically but she also has a loving dedicated relationship with God the Father. She continues to pray for healing in her relationship with her husband.

Probably every doctor would tell you in a moment of truth that they have a number of patients whose only real problem is that they are alone and they feel lonely. Out of a desire for attention they manifest all sorts of disease symptoms. It is really vital to examine your heart and your mind, looking for any hidden benefit you might get from sickness. In order to break free from this pattern, if you realize that you have been deriving any of these benefits from your illness, you need to face the truth that you have been paying too high a price.

Have you surrendered to your illness? Have you resigned yourself to an afflicted life, without realizing that you have yielded to an evil onslaught? Would you now be willing to no longer be resigned? Are you now willing to completely give up any trace of the self-pitying attitude of the victim? In short, do you want to get well? We need to be committed to the desire to be made whole.

"Illness, like war, is ten percent fear and pain and ninety per cent frustrating boredom." George and Cornelia Kay

A young woman showed up at our healing service. She was attractive but her looks could not hide the tension in her that simmered close to the surface. It also was not hard to guess that she had an eating disorder. She told us how for several months every time she had passed the church on her evening walks she heard an inner voice beckoning her to go in and pray. But she had resisted this voice. She said that she was 'spiritual but not Christian'. A close friend also strongly encouraged her to go to the healing service and she finally yielded to these two pressures and came to see if this could help her. The doctors had been unable to find what was wrong with her. However she was not getting any better. She was getting thinner and was constantly in pain throughout her whole body and she had no energy at all. We prayed for her and she was obviously moved. She started to attend regularly.

Over the next couple of visits to the church she told us more about herself. She explained that she had been rejected by a man she loved very much and had hoped to marry. Shortly after that, because she was too upset to pay attention she got into an accident and wrecked her car. She was in a great deal of pain physically and emotionally. She had lost her will to live and had been seriously contemplating suicide. The healing services gave her hope. One day things really took a turn for the better for her when she apologized to God for having wanted to take her life. She declared that she wanted to live again. From then on her healing accelerated. The physical pain diminished and she snapped out of her depression. Some energy returned and she was able to resume work. Outwardly she had lost a lot of tension, gained a little weight and looked marvelous. Inwardly she stopped saying that she was 'spiritual but not a Christian', no longer seeing these as being in any way opposed to each other. She started to openly profess her faith, enthusiastically telling people about God healing her. She regularly prays for family, friends and anyone who wants God's touch on their life.

God's Rx:

Prayerfully ask God to take away your need for any side benefits of your sickness and ask him instead to comfort you inwardly with his Holy Spirit. It is vital that we desire absolutely to be made well, if we are to receive God's healing.

*   *   *

"Things never go so well that one should have no fear and never go so badly that you should have no hope!" Anonymous

Facing fear

Fear is one of the more significant obstacles to healing. Fear magnifies the present situation and makes it even more dreadful than it actually is. Fear is an attitude of expecting the worst. Of course there are situations in life where fear is an appropriate response, warning us to get away from danger. But chronic fear is decidedly unhealthy. Fear blocks the flow of healing power. It pushes faith away from our hearts and our minds.

"Fear is a locked door which must be opened before anything else within the person can be healed." His Healing Touch. Monsignor Michael Buckley

God's word about fear is clear. Jesus said: **"Do not let your hearts be troubled and do not be afraid."** (John 14:27). God says: **"perfect love drives out fear."** (1 John 4:18). We know who can provide that perfect love—God Himself. St.Paul wrote: **"For God did not give us a spirit of fear, but a spirit of power, of love and of self-discipline."** (2 Timothy 1:7)

If you are being guided by fear, you are not being guided by God. In the final analysis, living in fear shows a lack of trust in God. Whether we are afraid of being in pain, afraid of long term illness or afraid of dying, fear is something which we need to acknowledge to God. We need to ask our Father God to take our fears from us.

There is therapy for fear. It begins with worshipping God and associating with people who know that in Christ there is victory over fear. We really need to learn to trust God. We need to ask him in prayer to help us overcome our unhealthy fears.

Scared to death

A very active sixty-five year old woman regularly attended our church. Her love for God was evident. She had a part-time position as a nurse at the hospice. She had remarked several times how dreadful it was to watch the many people who were wasting away in the last stages of cancer. She would ask them if they would like prayer and they almost always said 'yes'. She felt that she had a special ministry to comfort patients and their families in the last days of life. But seeing so many people dying was not an easy thing for her to bear and it exacted quite a toll on her emotionally and psychologically.

She developed some problems with pain and restriction of motion in one elbow and followed her doctor's recommendation to have surgery. It was a simple outpatient procedure. She was also given further tests on the same day, 'just as a routine check.' She was told she would be able to resume her nursing duties in a couple of days. When she got home that day there was an anxious sounding message from her doctor on the answering machine. He said she must call immediately. The tests had apparently revealed a tumor on her lung that looked malignant. The doctor wasn't in when she tried to return his call. She was very distressed and she called me and asked if I could meet her immediately. I told her to meet me at the church. She arrived there two minutes after I did. As I greeted her at the door I could see that there was already a look of resignation in her eyes. She started to cry and said she hoped that God would take her quickly. She was very adamant that she would not have to linger long in pain. She was also worried that she would be a burden on her family and she did not want to drain their finances. We prayed and I did my best to comfort her. On her return home there were several urgent messages from the doctor. He was terribly sorry. There had been a mix-up at the hospital and they were not her test results but someone else's that showed the cancer! She called me at home to tell me what the doctor had said. I said that was wonderful and that she must be very relieved. There was an odd silence on the line. I said again that it was great news and a tremendous relief. Then she said that she wasn't at all relieved. She was sure that the doctor was just saying that to try to soften the blow and to make her feel better. I said I was sure that could not be true and that as soon as she could talk to the doctor directly he would be able to answer any questions she might have and put her mind at ease. But in spite of the doctor's profuse apologies and insistence that there had been a mix-up and she did not have any sign of cancer, she never believed his reassurances.

Over the next few weeks I noticed her become thinner, paler and more depressed. She gave up her job, which was work she had loved. She gave up her church attendance and she withdrew more and more from her family. I visited her from time to time and kept in touch with her husband, who was very disconcerted by her behavior. He reported how she was constantly depressed and that she had little interest in eating and spent most of the time in bed. When I returned from a two week vacation I found that she had been admitted to hospital. I was shocked to see that she had become a shadow of her former self. Eight months had gone by since the initial mistaken diagnosis of cancer and now she had a confirmed, positive diagnosis of lung cancer. As I sat next to her and held her hand, she said with resignation, "I told you the doctor had just tried to protect me and that I had cancer all along." Two months later I officiated at her funeral. I have often wondered how much this condition was brought about as an effect of her fear and anxiety. It seemed as if her fears and the doctor's initial mistake had a severely detrimental effect on her will to live and resulted in her dying prematurely.

God's Rx:

If you are fearful, tell God the truth about your fear and ask him to take your fear away. Tell him you are sorry for not having trusted him and ask him to forgive you for that lack of trust. Then tell God you are now putting your trust in him and you want to live your life consistent with that trust. Know that he will send his Holy Spirit to give you peace of mind. His Spirit will give you the inner strength to rise above your deepest fears.

*　　　　　*　　　　　*

Is death the end of the road?

"Fear not that thy life shall come to an end, but rather fear that it shall never have a beginning." Cardinal John Newman

The ultimate fear for most people is death. Psychologists are agreed on this point. Death has been humanity's enemy since the dawn of time. We decorate it with flowers, soften it with speeches and shroud it with noble sounding metaphors, but dead is still dead and it's scary. Death invariably strikes as a catastrophe whenever we encounter it, whether it is in an automobile accident, through disease, through violence, through suicide, in a war, in youth or in old age.

In an attempt to take away the sting of death many people have turned to the East and embraced the theory of reincarnation as an explanation. According to this understanding, we exit through one door, discarding our old bodies, only to reenter the planet in a different body for round seven hundred and sixty-nine, just one more trip on the wheel of life. This is a very costly escape into self deception. The Christian view provides a stark contrast to this idea. The Bible tells us that we have only one life here and this is it: **"man is destined to die once, and after that to face judgment."** (Hebrews 9:27)

The aim of healing is not, of course, to postpone death indefinitely. The aim of healing is to bring people to wholeness. Ultimately the most important healing is the reconciling and reuniting of our soul with God the Father and the personal commitment of our life to Jesus Christ as our Savior and Lord.

In the most well-known prayer Jesus taught us to say: "**Thy will be done, Thy Kingdom come, as it is in Heaven.**" As it is in Heaven, where there is no fear and where God's peace is never violated by death. As it is in Heaven, where God's perfect ways have not been defiled by evil. Jesus told us to pray for the coming of this new kingdom, and the passing away of the old world, where sickness, decay and death dominate. They are our constant reminders that we human beings have not lived according to God's will.

Jesus said, "**I am the resurrection and the life. He who believes in me will live, even though he dies, and whoever lives and believes in me will never die.**" (**John 11:25,26**). The Bible makes it clear that if we trust in the Lord we will live for ever. We were created to be eternal. Yes, we must each meet death and yes, the statistics on death are impressive, holding steady at one hundred per cent of the population. But death is not the end. Because of Jesus's sacrificial substitution of himself on the cross, death has lost its terminal bite. According to God, death is no longer a permanent condition for those who believe in him. It is now merely a transition to life in his eternal kingdom. So with that much hanging in the balance it becomes vitally important for each of us to be clear on our answer to the question: "Do I believe in God?"

Anxiety and Doubt

"**Worry affects the circulation, the glands, the whole nervous system and profoundly affects the heart. I have never known a man who died from overwork, but I have known some who died from doubt.**" Dr. **Norman Douglas**

In asking God for healing we should not be weighed down with anxiety or confusion. Our anxiety can block the flow of healing. We may pray earnestly and long and even declare our faith in God's word that we will be healed. Then, in our weaker moments we doubt God's ability to heal. We question whether or not he even hears us. This undermines our faith and we need to guard our minds against such doubts. So we need to honestly express our anxieties and confusion to God, bringing them to him and asking him to deal with them. We need to ask God to make us open to receive his healing touch. Then we need to encourage ourselves frequently with positive affirmations of God's love for us. We can give ourselves positive self-talk, reminding ourselves of his power and his desire to heal each and every one of us.

"A cheerful heart is good medicine" Proverbs 17:22

One day at a healing service I talked about the need to believe God and to claim faith. We cannot hope our way into faith. We have to seize it. We need to believe in the healing we are receiving before we see the results. We need to affirm to ourselves positive thoughts about getting healed. At the end of the service I saw one woman had the letters IAH written in ball-point pen on her arm. I asked her what that was supposed to mean. She said that she believed she had received a healing touch from God and she was going to keep on affirming that to herself. So she wrote the letters IAH to remind herself "I Am Healed." Even though she has been engaged in a battle against a pituitary growth she continues to maintain an optimistic outlook and give thanks for her healing.

"Doubt makes the mountain which faith can move." Anonymous

You can do anything

Look around you for people who seem to be genuinely content or happy. If you know anyone who appears truly contented you might also notice that usually their lives are not outwardly apparently any 'better' than anyone else's. They experience much the same strange mixture of sad and happy events that most people experience. Yet they find the ability to retain a sense of humor even in the most trying of circumstances. They manage to find pleasure in the small and simple things of life. The ability to be joyful, in spite of difficulties, is something we can intentionally cultivate within ourselves. As St.Paul wrote: **"I have learned the secret of** being content in any and every situation, whether well fed or hungry, whether living in plenty or in want. I can do everything through him who gives me strength." (Philippians 4:12-13)

God's Rx:

Intentionally cultivate an attitude of inner contentment.
"A cheerful heart is good medicine." (Proverbs 17:22)
Remember the song: "Don't worry. Be happy."

*   *   *

"I've been bad!"—The Big Time-out!

"I'm being punished for what I did! That's why I'm so sick. God is angry at me. He will never forgive me for what I have done." You would be surprised at how many people entertain such thoughts.

"God wants us to be victors not victims, to grow not grovel, to soar not sink, to overcome, not to be overwhelmed." W. Ward

All modern parents are familiar with the idea of time-out. Their children have been naughty and the parents think they need time for reflection. So they get time out. What the parents don't do is say, "OK kid, you've been really bad, so I'm going to give you the mumps." So why would we, the children of God, imagine that our heavenly Father is so mean? What an extraordinary idea it is, to blame our suffering on God! But, time and again, we hear from people that they think that God is 'doing it to them.'

When God's son Jesus Christ walked the earth, he spent the majority of his time taking away the sufferings of the people. Nowhere in the New Testament do you find Jesus punishing people by inflicting suffering on them. Granted, there is talk in the Bible about God punishing the wicked, but it is always with the promise that if people will turn from their selfish ways to Him that he will forgive them and renew them. For example, God says: **'If my people who are called by my name, will humble themselves and pray and seek my face and turn from their wicked ways, then I will** hear from Heaven and will forgive their sin and heal their land." (2 Chronicles 7:14)

We need to realize, once and for always, that God is not interested in inflicting punishment arbitrarily on his people. However he is definitely interested in discipline. Discipline is the work of the Holy Spirit to show us right from wrong, to develop in us an awareness of sin and a genuine distaste for it. Discipline is the work of the Holy Spirit to purify our spirit and strengthen our character. So do not imagine that God has put you in some kind of permanent divine time out. There is nothing that God will not forgive.

"Those who I love, I rebuke and discipline. So be earnest and repent. Here I am. I stand at the door and knock. If anyone hears my voice and opens the door, I will come in and eat with him and he with me." (Revelation 3:19,20)

God's Rx:

If you have in your mind the memory of something you have done wrong, and you fear that God is punishing you for it, there is a perfect remedy. Confess to God what you have done wrong and apologize to him from the bottom of your heart. Then ask him for his forgiveness and know that he does forgive you. He forgives you completely. Be open to accepting his forgiveness graciously. Jesus came to offer us all God's perfect and complete forgiveness.

*   *   *

Life—God's Boot Camp

Discipline is not a popular idea these days. A lot of people in the twenty-first century cannot see the connection between discipline and love. Discipline means the training of the disciple. As we have already pointed out, God does not arbitrarily inflict illness on us to discipline us. But he will use the illnesses and troubles that we have, as a means of teaching us.

God will use all the circumstances of life to teach his children, whether in times of joy or sadness or sickness or death or new life. Through his Holy Spirit, he can touch all the events of our lives in this broken world. Thus out of sickness, tragedy and even death, magnificent lessons in God's grace have been learned.

By disciplining us, God is educating our spirits and our minds, making us stronger and more faithful for his use. He uses the problems we may have with our life and our health to assist in this process of our education. They are not a punishment. Do not try to make God guilty of causing you suffering. You will only make it harder to receive the comfort and healing that God wants to give you.

CHAPTER SEVEN

▼

THERE IS POWER IN THEOLOGY

(Theos = God. Theology = thinking about God)

A lot of people find theological thought to be dry and dull and hard to read. Regrettably a great number of theological books fall into that category. However there are some key theological truths which, once you understand them clearly, can make an enormously powerful difference. Understanding the theology of 'atonement' is amazingly liberating.

Understanding Atonement

According to the Oxford dictionary, to 'atone' means to make amends, or to make up for some error or deficiency. Some readers may find this teaching of 'atonement' to be a departure from the view of a vindictive God who punishes people on the spot for their sins. God the Father offers his people true comfort through the incarnation of his Son our Lord Jesus Christ. The Christ became the man Jesus, to bear sorrow, sickness, grief, sin and even death for all people.

In his death he killed off the root cause of all suffering, by breaking the power of sin. By his resurrection, which was the complete victory over death, Jesus redeemed humanity and brought back true goodness across the endless chaos and suffering of our sin. In this act of atonement on the cross, God was in Jesus, reconciling the world to himself. Do you realize that it was also for you that he suffered? Do you realize, as the Scripture tells us, that he took on the sins of the world, that 'he was bruised for our iniquities and that by his wounds we are healed'? This is how the death of Jesus relates to our personal sin. He brought reconciliation, not just to a select few, but to the whole world, to whoever would believe in him.

"This is how God showed his love among us: He sent his one and only Son into the world that we might live through him. This is love: not that we loved God, but that he loved us and sent his Son as an atoning sacrifice for our sins." (1 John 4:7)

To think that God is punishing us shows a complete misunderstanding of the nature of God's love for us and discredits this infinitely powerful atonement that Jesus Christ made for us, on the cross.

"The intimate relations which exist between obedience and health, between sanctification, which is the health of the soul and the divine healing which insures the health of the body—both are comprised in salvation that comes from God." Divine Healing. Andrew Murray

God's Rx:

Ask God to forgive you for ever doubting his love for you and for all humankind. Ask him to completely restore your Father—child relationship with him.

CHAPTER EIGHT

▼

I FOUGHT THE LAW AND THE LAW WON!

"Be very careful, then, how you live, not as unwise but as wise, making the most of every opportunity, because the days are evil. Therefore do not be foolish, but understand what the Lord's will is." (Ephesians 5:15).

This book you are reading is not the complete guide to the will of God for his children. For that we need to engage in the consistent study of the Holy Bible, where God the Father's Will and Testament is recorded. At the same time we need to ask the Holy Spirit to guide us in discovering God's perfect will for our personal lives. Exploring the will of God brings us compellingly back to the healing place of a real connection with God, our Creator and Father. It also helps to increase our understanding of, and faith in, the healing work of our Lord Jesus Christ.

"Those who go against the grain of God's laws should not complain when they get splinters." Arkansas Methodist

Spiritual laws, like physical laws, must be respected in order for them to work for you. For example, the requirement for sleep is a physical law you cannot ignore for long before it catches up with you. Jesus Christ said: "If

you abide in me and my words remain in you, ask whatever you wish, and it will be given you. This is to my Father's glory, that you bear much fruit, showing yourselves to be my disciples." (John 15:7,8). This is a spiritual law.

To break it down, seeing God's will is threefold. Firstly, to abide in Christ means to believe that Jesus is the Christ, the Son of God, who was sent to bring salvation and wholeness to mankind. Secondly, to abide in his words is to know what he taught and to live the life he taught and demonstrated. This includes asking forgiveness for our pride, envy, resentment, selfishness, greed, lust, anger and evil thoughts. Thirdly, he tells us the magnificent result of knowing and living according to his will for our lives: **"ask whatever you wish, and it will be given you."** We ask in prayer for healing for ourselves and those we love. When we are abiding in his Word and living according to his will, this is a spiritual law well worth remembering: **"If you abide in me and my words remain in you, ask whatever you wish, and it will be given you. This is to my Father's glory, that you bear much fruit, showing yourselves to be my disciples."** (John 15:7,8)

I'm sorry! I'm sorry! I'll clean it all up. I promise!

As you can see, we all need to do a thorough clean up operation on our lives. The Word of God tells us that we must let our old self, which is our selfish nature, die. God's will for you may not be the same as what you think you want for yourself. God's will and your personal will can even be in direct opposition. Would you now be willing to turn your self-willfulness over to Christ? Of course, God, being God, can do anything he wants. But it is a good general rule to say that he requires our cooperation to make changes in our lives. Any medical doctor would require the same. No doctor would expect their patient to recover if they refused to follow the doctor's advice and refused to take their prescribed medications. The person diagnosed with emphysema is told, "you must stop smoking immediately or you will end up on a respirator." Their refusal to quit smoking is violating the physical law.

There is a price to pay sooner or later for breaking physical laws. Equally so there are spiritual laws, things required by God, that we all need to comply with, in order to bring ourselves in line with his healing will. These laws relate to our conduct and to forgiveness of others. When we have violated these laws, we need to make a new commitment to obedience. God's words are our final authority.

"We have 35 million laws trying to enforce the Ten Commandments!" **Earl Wilson**

The New Testament does not record that Jesus was ever sick. Might that have been because he lived in continuous communion with God, his Father and he always obeyed God's perfect laws for life and health?

God's Rx:

Resolve now to stop violating both the physical laws of health and the spiritual laws of God.

The vital importance of Forgiveness

"Love your enemy and it will completely confuse him!" **Anonymous**

Because of our pride and selfishness we have a difficult time admitting our sins and asking God for forgiveness. Then when it comes to forgiving others we wonder how we could forgive them. We say, "I can't forgive them because after all, they did…to me; and they said…! I just can't condone their behavior…and what's more I don't think they should be allowed to get away with it." But there is a heavy price to pay for refusing to forgive. Unforgiveness increases discontent in ourselves. It erodes our emotional well-being and causes our health to deteriorate. Did you know that unforgiveness is itself a sin? Through the sin of unforgiveness we are alienated from our Father God and from meaningful relationships with other people.

"Life's difficulties are intended to make us better not bitter." **Anonymous**

All of us have suffered wrongful treatment both by people close to us and by strangers. God wants us to be freed from the stress of holding on to pain and resentment from the past.

"Delight your soul and comfort your heart. Remove sorrow far from you, for sorrow has destroyed many and there is no profit in it." (Ecclesiasticus 30:23)

It is a helpful idea to list all the people who have harmed us and ask God to help us to forgive them. Left to our own devices we are extremely unlikely to want to forgive anyone. But God can take away our unforgiving nature and give us the compassion and true strength of character that makes us able to forgive people. When we forgive others it is amazing how much pain disappears from our own bodies.

"There is much from our past that continues to affect us negatively today—physically, emotionally and spiritually. As we bring these hurts before the Lord, we can be set free to be the people we want to be and God wants us to be." Christian Healing. Mark Pearson

God's Rx:

Please become a forgiving person. Forgiveness heals relationships and individuals. When we forgive others it is amazing how much pain disappears from our own bodies.

           *   *   *

First things first

"If you are offering your gift at the altar and there remember that your brother has something against you, leave your gift there in front of the altar. First go and be reconciled to your brother; then come and offer your gift." Matthew 5:23,24

At a healing conference in Northern California we devoted the Saturday afternoon to the role of forgiveness in healing. Toward the end of the session we asked the participants to come forward to the altar rail for prayer, with a willingness to release the person they needed to forgive and to ask God's help with forgiveness. Earlier we had both been aware of a well-dressed woman in her late forties who sat stiffly and whose body and face seemed rigid with suppressed anger. As everyone else lined up to release their unforgiveness before God and to forgive the people for whom they were holding resentment this woman did not move an inch. Instead she became even more rigid.

Khara walked over and sat next to her. She asked her if there was someone that she thought she needed to forgive. Through tight lips she said in crisp tones, "I am not angry with anyone and I am not the kind of person who holds grudges." Khara could not accept her answer and continued, "None of us can get through life without getting hurt or feeling let down or betrayed by someone. Surely there must be someone." As Khara put her arm around this woman's shoulders she suddenly broke into uncontrollable sobbing. Through the sobs and the tears she said, "Well there was my husband, Bill. He treated me so awfully. Then my sister Mary would always turn my mother against me." As she and Khara moved together towards the altar the names kept coming. She blurted out the names of about forty people who had hurt her and who until that moment she had never been able to forgive. We watched in astonishment as her face quite suddenly softened and a relaxation spread through her body. It was as though the suppressed pain, anger and resentment had been the starch that had held her face and body in that stiff, rigid state.

The physical transformation was instantaneous as she seemed to shed years and her tears became interspersed with laughter. Through one hour of confession, tears and prayer a soft and funny woman was healed of anger, resentment and unforgiveness right before our very eyes. We later learned from her that in subsequent nights she suddenly found that she slept deeply and peacefully the whole night through, something she had not experienced in many years.

"You can prepare for him a highway that he may come more quickly. You can clear that highway by removing the rocks of resentment towards

others that tend to accumulate over the years. And this you do by an act of forgiveness." The Healing Gifts of the Spirit. Agnes Sanford

The soul heals through allowing forgiveness to flow in and out. Forgiveness mends the damage from painful memories and heals the shattered emotions. It sets the stage for healing the body of illness.

God is green—Natural Laws

Natural laws are God's laws for the welfare of mankind. When we are able to conform to these laws we are more likely to find ourselves well and content. The laws of nature have not broken humanity. Human beings have broken themselves against the laws of nature. We cannot break God's laws to suit the self-serving desires of the fallen human race without reaping the consequences. For example, one of the many terrible consequences of widespread greed is industrial pollution in our rivers. Another consequence is the use of excessive chemical additives being put into our food in order to promote shelf life and profitability at the expense of good nutrition and health. So some of the water and the food, that God provided to sustain us all, ends up having a detrimental effect on our health.

God's Rx:

Use the wisdom God gave you.
Pay attention to what you eat, breathe and drink.

                    *   *   *

"Just take it all away!"

If we convinced God to suspend his natural laws, so that sin and misuse of our bodies and the misuse of our natural resources had no consequence, what would happen to the moral nature of humanity? How corrupt is our society already because God's laws are being ignored? How much more would man's inhumanity to man increase, if there was no consequence for breaking God's laws?

"Do not be deceived: God cannot be mocked. A man reaps what he sows. The one who sows to please his sinful nature, from that nature will reap destruction; the one who sows to please the Spirit, from the Spirit will reap eternal life." (Galatians 6:7,8)

This law operates equally either way, for happiness or for misery. The inevitable outcome of abusing God's natural laws is the suffering, sorrow, sickness and death which transpire in our world. These are the natural consequences which occur in the world as a function of our collective physical and mental abuse of God's natural law, or to put it another way, the consequences of our innumerable wrong uses of right things. What would it mean for us if God prevented all suffering? He would have to overturn his spiritual and natural laws, and put an end to the freewill that he gave us. Discord and disorder are not the work of God. They are the direct natural result of man's misuse of God's natural laws. Don't let the devil tempt us once again with the false hope of escape from the natural and inevitable consequences of sin, as he originally did with Adam and Eve, saying in effect: "Go ahead, do it your way, not God's. Nothing bad will happen to you."

God's Rx:

When you know you have been in error, you need to do a complete 'about face'. It's time to change your ways of thinking and acting.

*   *   *

"May the Source be with you!"—Spiritual Healing

"If God is kept outside, there is something wrong inside." Anonymous

In researching for our own health and for this book we have found that sickness is essentially a spiritual condition. That is to say that underlying the physical conditions and manifestations of sickness, there is a spiritual condition which needs to be addressed. Dr. Carl Jung, one of the key figures in psychology, said that, **"healing may be a religious problem."**

We believe that God is always central to healing. He heals through his Spirit. Healing starts in the human spirit and it moves where it is needed in the mind or the body. There are people who, for their own confused reasons, want God's healing without God. They criticize religion and make fun of people who believe. But religion literally means to bind back to our source and what is our source if it is not God? We know that God's spiritual laws work. He made them to bring us out of the state of separation from him. By obeying the spiritual laws of God, we become connected back to our source, who is God our Father. This allows us to be healed in body, mind and spirit.

"We should keep up in our hearts a constant sense of our own weakness, not with a design to discourage the mind and depress the spirit, but with a view to drive us out of ourselves in search of divine assistance." Practical Piety. Hannah Moore

God's Rx:

Remember this: **Jesus said, "As the Father has loved me, so have I loved you. Now remain in my love. If you obey my commands, you will remain in my love, just as I have obeyed my Father's commands and remain in his love. I have told you this so that my joy may be in you and so that your joy may be complete." (John 15:9-11)**

*   *   *

What's sin got to do with it?

"You cannot play with sin and overcome it at the same time." J. D. Macaulay

The Bible teaches us that all sickness originated in sin and that Satan is the author of all that is sinful, all that is ill and all that is evil. Sin is basically just selfishness. Sin is defined as being the state of separation from God. It is the state of feeling disconnected and out of touch with God. Sins, plural, are specific behaviors or ways of thinking that keep us separated from God.

The consequences of sin in this life are suffering, sickness and death. The good news is that the consequence of God's forgiveness is the ultimate release from suffering, sickness and death. God's forgiveness brings healing. It absolves the soul, it frees the worried mind and it cleanses and renews the spirit. This alone has an enormously powerful, beneficial effect on the body.

"We discover and experience release from our guilt in direct proportion to our willingness to face our sin, confess our sinfulness and accept forgiveness." The Freedom of Forgiveness. David Augsburger

Adverse spiritual conditions

It is clear that Jesus himself saw sickness as being a spiritual enemy. The Scriptures record:

"how God anointed Jesus of Nazareth with the Holy Spirit and power, and how he went around doing good and healing all who were under the power of the devil, because God was with him." (Acts 10:38). Disease is an adverse spiritual condition, whose origin is the devil and for which Christ is the antidote. Disease yields to the perfect will of God.

We read several times in the Bible how Jesus rebuked spirits that were tormenting people's mental state and how he rebuked fever. On these occasions, Jesus was speaking directly to the adverse spiritual condition, ordering it to 'let go' and 'get out.' St. Paul cautioned us that, **"our struggle is not against flesh and blood, but against the rulers, against the authorities against the powers of this dark world and against the spiritual forces of evil."** He continues: **"Therefore, put on the full armor of God, so that when the day of evil comes, you may be able to stand your ground, and after you have done everything, to stand."** (Ephesians 6:12,13)

▼

CHAPTER NINE

CONSIDER IT DONE!—GOD'S PROVISION FOR HEALING

Thankfully for us, God has provided for our healing. The following passage of Scripture gives us tremendous assurance. The prophet Isaiah wrote: **"Surely he took up our infirmities and carried our sorrows. Yet we considered him stricken by God, smitten by him and afflicted. But he was pierced for our transgressions; he was crushed for our iniquities, the punishment that brought us peace was laid upon him and by his wounds we are healed."** (Isaiah 53:4-6). In another translation (Young), this reads, **"Surely he has born our sicknesses and he has carried our pains."** This is not intended just to mean that he experienced the full range of human sufferings. This has infinitely greater significance.

It states clearly that he died for our healing and our peace, to relieve us of our sickness, our pain and the widespread effect of sin. He took upon himself the sufferings that we were destined to bear and that we deserved. It means that he personally endured suffering and death in order to liberate us from them. This is vitally important to understand! It is hard to grasp the enormous significance of this and you may need to reread it and pray about it and reflect on it. For many people this is a radical and profound transformation of our thinking on divine healing. There are people who have experienced a complete physical recovery from chronic illness, simply from having come to this understanding that God made provision for our healing.

"It is very difficult for him (the Holy Spirit) to hold you if you are struggling, fighting and striving. Just relax and rest in the Lord." Peace with God. Billy Graham.

God's Rx:

Remember that God has made provision for your healing. Claim your birthrights as a child of God.

*   *   *

The Cross, Redemption and Health

"Other men see only a hopeless end, but the Christian rejoices in an endless hope." Anonymous

Healing is an integral, central part of Christ's redeeming work. The word 'vicariously' means in our place. Christ vicariously bore our sins and iniquities on the cross. He vicariously bore our illnesses and our pains. The Apostle Peter makes this same crucial point, when he says in his first letter, **"he himself bore our sins in his body on the tree so that we might die to sins and live for righteousness. By his wounds, you have been healed." (1 Peter 2:24).** We need to begin to exercise our faith, by appropriating for ourselves this provision that God has made for our healing, for our wholeness.

When this powerful concept becomes clear in our minds and dawns in our spirit, the Holy Spirit will begin to manifest a different reality in our life. The point is that Christ came to redeem us from both sin and sickness.

Understanding this helps us to understand the story of Jesus healing a man suffering from paralysis. First he forgave him. Then he healed him. '**When Jesus saw their faith, he said: "Friend, your sins are forgiven."' And then, seeing the people become angry at his saying this, he said to them, "Why are you thinking about these things in your heart? Which is easier to say, 'your sins are forgiven', or to say, 'Get up and walk?' But that you may know that the Son of Man has authority on earth to forgive sins…" He said to the paralyzed man, "I tell you get up, take your mat and go home." Immediately he stood up in front of them, took what he had been lying on and went home, praising God.' (Luke 5:20-25).** It is clear that God's forgiveness for our sins and the healing of sickness are connected. Jesus gave authority for his followers, for everyone who believes in him, to heal the sick and cast out devils.

God's Rx:

Raise your readiness to receive healing, through believing in Jesus Christ's purpose here on earth and by accepting God's forgiveness for your sins.

*   *   *

Removing the road blocks on the journey to wholeness and health

"Christian love, either towards God or towards man is an affair of the will." Mere Christianity. C.S. Lewis

Anything that separates you from God is a road block on the path to receiving divine healing. It is an obstacle to God's power and to your health. We need to eliminate these obstacles from our lives or at least learn to manage them better. Let's clear these blocks away…

Obstacles to healing

Negativity

Get rid of negativity. Yours. Your friend's or a member of your family or medical staff. Let go and let God. Your friends may think you are crazy, but the Lord is on your side. Feed your mind with encouragement from Scripture.

No prayer life

You 'don't have the time.' You can't ask people to pray for you. Too proud? Too ashamed? Give it up! Show a little humility before God and open yourself up to the power of prayer. Exercise your knees.

The need to be sick

You like the extra attention that being sick has got you. But your sickness has become a part of who you are! You have become your ailment.

Stop exploiting your condition for extra sympathy. The attention you need most is from God and he loves you more than you can imagine.

Ignoring God's will

"I don't have time to read the Bible. What could that have to do with anything anyway? What can some very dated and old fashioned book tell me about my health and my life?"

Read it and find out. Pray that God will show you everything that he wants you to learn.

Wise and healthy choices

Bad diet. Prescription or recreational drug dependency. Drinking too much. Smoking too much. TV addiction. Worrying too much.

Ask God to fill you with his Holy Spirit and to strengthen your will so that you can rise above what used to drag you down.

Bad attitude

'I'm wounded. I can't let go of the pain. I can't see myself ever getting better. I guess it's God's will that I'm sick. It's hopeless!'

Your focus is on your illness, not on God. Tell God honestly about the trouble you are having with your attitude. Ask him to heal and adjust your attitude. Get out of the pity chair and give up being a victim.

Unbelief

'I don't have any faith. I'm just not that kind of person!' Remember that Faith is a gift from God. Ask him for that gift of faith. The squeaky wheel gets oiled. Ask him for faith and then immediately start thanking him for building your faith. Let go and let God.

Unforgiving

'I can't forgive them for what they did. I'll never forgive them!'

Is unforgiveness poisoning you? Don't let your pride and anger hurt you.

Ask God to help you to forgive. Then in prayer try saying: 'I forgive (name).'

Repeat as often as necessary. Keep saying it till you mean it.

No repentance

'I don't see why I need to repent. I'm a good person.'

Maybe you are. But none of us are perfect and we have all fallen short in more ways than we care to remember and we all have sinned in the eyes of God. So, "on your knees, brothers and sisters!" Ask God to show you where you are wrong, admit it to him and ask for the strength to change it.

Fear

'I'm scared to death!'

Yes, you and a few million others. Fear kills. This is a big obstacle. There is only one direction to turn that will help you to rise above fear. There is only one person who can help you to transcend fear and that is the Lord Jesus Christ. Remember that **"perfect love casts out fear."** (1 John 4:18)

Some of the obstacles to healing are listed above. There may well be more, varying from person to person. It is extremely helpful to ask God to show you any other obstacles you might have to your healing journey. As you become more aware what the obstacles on your path to healing are, you can begin to let go of them.

Repaving the road to health—Always keep a positive outlook

Some Do's and Don'ts

- Pray for others
- Pray for yourself
- Be thankful
- Don't live in the past
- Use the stumbling blocks of life as stepping stones
- Remember you are not your illness
- Do something kind for someone else
- Don't talk about sickness at meals
- Laugh
- Make other people laugh
- Learn to forgive ASAP
- Refuse to be possessed by your possessions
- Get plenty of fresh air
- Don't gossip
- Seek out beauty
- Don't reinforce your illness by continually discussing it
- Don't be afraid of change
- Set achievable goals
- Count your blessings
- Listen to music that soothes your nerves
- Develop your sense of humor
- Don't let doctors make a living off your bad habits
- Relax
- Learn to play again
- Keep your chin up and your knees down

CHAPTER TEN

▼

THAT NOT SO ORGANIZED RELIGION

Is your church focused on healing? Do you attend a church that offers a healing service? When we look back at Jesus's earthly ministry, it is apparent that the magnet that made so many people follow him was healing. We read in the Bible how, **"Jesus told his disciples to have a boat ready for him to keep the people from crowding him, for he had healed many, so that those with diseases were pushing forward to touch him." (Mark 3:9).** One sixth of the gospels are devoted to stories about Jesus miraculously healing people.

In the letter of James to the Church, he writes, **"Is any one of you sick? He should call the elders of the church to pray over him and anoint him with oil in the name of the Lord. And the prayer offered in faith will make the sick person well. The Lord will raise him up." (James 5:14-16).** This verse of Scripture is God's teaching on seeking his healing. It points to a veritable tool chest for healing.

"Offering prayers for healing to the community is a ministry that demonstrates the compassion of Christ." Praying for wholeness and healing. Richard J. Beckmen

There are plenty of churches and ministries today where our Lord's healing ministry is offered and where the clergy and other members are willing and ready to pray for you. Unfortunately though, many church leaders today do not offer healing services. They do not encourage the laying on of hands or anointing with oil for healing.

"We give people a dose of religion when they are looking for an encounter with the living God!" Kenneth Pillar

Even if your church does not offer a healing ministry you can ask your priest or pastor to pray for your healing, to lay hands on you and anoint you with oil, as the Bible instructs. You can ask your minister to pray with you for someone you care for. You can ask him or her to bless your medication in the name of the Lord. If this is uncharted territory for them it may be a great blessing for them to discover for themself the healing love and power of God at work. On the other hand, they may say that they do not believe that God has healed anyone since the time of the apostles in the first century! In which case you may need to seek out a church where healing prayer support is offered. There are many churches where the minister and the people believe that the Lord is alive and that he heals today. The Order of St.Luke is an international network of people and church groups dedicated to the ministry of Christian healing. There may be a group in your area. (See the back of the book for further information.)

"Both the laying-on of hands and anointing with oil have proved to be enormously effective channels for the healing power of the Holy Spirit." Celebration of healing. Emily Gardiner Neal

In our healing ministry we have found that true corporate prayer, where together we really hold one another up to God for healing, is incredibly powerful. In this kind of atmosphere, where people join together to pray in spirit and in truth, Church can be a place where fear is conquered, loneliness is overcome, spiritual and psychological burdens are lifted and healing occurs. In such a church a new way is discovered, where you learn to walk faithfully with Christ. This is spiritual therapy, where you experience the healing love of Christ flowing into your life through his body, the Church. Go to a church, but don't just go there. Participate actively in the worship of God. As you do so you can feel the praise and thanksgiving to God cleansing and purifying you.

"Every Christian community is a healing community for itself, for the church and for the world." His healing touch. Monsignor Michael Buckley

"Praise the Lord, oh my soul. Praise the Lord who forgives all your sins and heals all your diseases." (Psalm 103:3)

If your church has a healing service take part in it. If your church offers Holy Communion or the Lord's Supper, receive it with the knowledge that God is nourishing your spirit. Discover for yourself how liberating it is to confess your sins to God. It washes away the guilt, lifts your spirits and balances your damaged emotions. David Augsburger expressed this well when he wrote: **"A moment of complete honesty, a moment when we come to a true confession of who and what we are is an eternal moment of truth." The freedom of forgiveness. David Augsburger**

God's Rx:

Find a healing Christian community.
Visit it. Become an active part of it.

CHAPTER ELEVEN

▼

FURNISHING YOUR TEMPLE

"Do you not know that your body is a temple of the Holy Spirit, who is in you, who you have received from God?…Therefore honor God with your body." (1 Corinthians 6:19-20)

How would you really like your home to be? Peaceful, loving, clean, comfortable? Perhaps with a beautiful view and decorated with magnificent furniture and fine works of art? Your body is a house that God wants to live in, where he wants his Spirit to be in residence. Take a look around your 'house'. Are you ready to invite him in? Or is a little personal house cleaning in order?

As we start to clean house let's start with our head. It seems that we are often unable to find peace. We become worried, anxious or depressed. We think we don't have enough time or energy to offer to our families, or to God or to church or to anything. We need the wounds from our past, as well as the present, to be healed. If we could find that "peace that passes understanding" by ourselves, through our own will, we would already have done so. We need to ask God to fill our hearts with his peace. Be willing to turn your pain, your problems and indeed every area of your life over to Jesus Christ, and let him do his work in your life. There are things in our lives that have robbed us of peace. They keep us worried and anxious. This constant internal irritation and anxiety contaminates our spirit, undermines our strength, and spreads sickness from our mind to our body. Maybe you don't know the exact cause of your dis-ease, but Christ has the remedy. Spiritual disease logically must have a spiritual remedy. Take the time to do a spiritual self-examination. Reflect and assess the causes of being ill at ease in your life and in your body. Write down the things, people and situations that rob you of your peace. Then bring them before God in prayer, telling him how you have been feeling and asking him to help you overcome negativity.

A young attractive woman, Carolyn was clearly under a cloud of sadness and pain. Her husband was diagnosed with manic depression and was on medication. She suffered from Graves disease and was often desperately fatigued. We invited them both to our Wednesday evening spiritual journey program. He dropped out after the first session as the discussion focused on how God loves us just the way we are but loves us too much to let us stay that way. Carolyn on the other hand immersed herself in the classes asking questions and interacting with a refreshing degree of openness and honesty. She shared about her health and marital difficulties. She quickly entered into a close personal relationship with God. She accepted with a childlike trust that he would bring healing to her. She soon began working four then five days a week instead of the three she had been limited to because of constant muscle weakness. Her medication was reduced and she could once again sleep well at night. Her personality changed dramatically as she blossomed into a joyful, positive and enthusiastic person who looked ten years younger than the woman we had first met. There was always a smile on her face and she loved sharing her faith and her healing with anyone who she encountered.

When we really embrace the idea that our body is the temple of God, it becomes very clear that there are a lot of things that we will have to change. We cannot help but notice things that are inappropriate in a spiritual temple. If a place is beautiful and the atmosphere is peaceful, would you spoil it by throwing garbage around? Of course not! Would you defile the temple with drugs or drunkenness, with excessive food consumption or gluttony that is harmful to the heart and other vital organs? When we look for causes of disease in our bodies and minds, it makes sense to look for unsanitary or contagious conditions. We need to ask ourselves whether we are living in accordance with the natural laws of right eating, rest and hygiene. Hygiene is a state of mind just as much as it is a condition of outer cleanliness. Are we willing to turn our attitudes, our thinking, our eating and our drinking habits over to God? Lack of forgiveness, jealousy, bitterness and resentment are like spiritual cholesterol blocking the lifeblood of the spirit. To be an acceptable temple of the Holy Spirit there needs to be a real cleaning up of our lives from the inside out. Good health is an inside job. We need to cooperate with God in keeping his temple clean.

"Nothing so needs reforming as other people's habits!" Mark Twain.

We may need to change a lifetime of bad habits to start living in accord with God. If, by the grace of God, we begin to experience healing but then go right back into the old habits that contributed to the illness, we are not moving in the direction of healing and wholeness, but away from it. If you go back into an unrepentant life, choosing the darkness of bitterness and blame, or staying fixated on fear and stress, you again set up the situations that were a contributing factor to your illness. This would be as insane as painting the walls of your home, then throwing dirt on the fresh paint.

Guess who's coming to dinner?

If your phone were to ring right now, and to your great surprise, God spoke to you personally, and said, "I will be at your home in one hour," what would you do? Rush around cleaning, tidying, throwing away things you are ashamed of, getting out your best china and silver, bringing out the finest food, and hope this would make a good impression! We need to really understand that we are not just inviting God over for a brief visit, but asking him to live in us, in our spirit, in our mind and in our body. He wants to share with us what we eat, drink, think, feel, read and experience. Are you ready for your special guest?

"Christian miracles...show invasion by a power which is not alien. They are what might be expected when she (the earth) is invaded not simply by a god but by The God of nature." Miracles. C.S. Lewis

God's Rx:

Prepare yourself through prayer and diligence to be a temple fit for the Spirit of God. In prayer and meditation see the Holy Spirit taking residence in your mind and body. He wants a clean house, so ask his help with those dirty inner cleaning jobs. Picture him moving away all harmful habits and dis-ease, so he can feel comfortably at home.

▼

CHAPTER TWELVE

GOD'S LAST WILL AND TESTAMENT

"Worship the Lord your God, and his blessing will be on your food and water. I will take away sickness from among you." (Exodus 23:25)

Imagine your surprise when you learn that you have been left an inheritance of immense value and you discover that a copy of the "last will and testament" is in a drawer. Would you leave it there unopened and unexamined? Wouldn't you be just a little curious about what has been left to you? Wouldn't you be excited about taking it out and reading it? There are gifts of immense value that God has left for us and they are recorded in his "Last Will and Testament," the Holy Bible.

O.K. I got the will! Now what else can I do?

"Never be afraid to trust an unknown future to the known God." Corrie Ten Boom

A lament we often hear is: "If God really wanted me well, he would heal me! He knows I want to be healed. I pray every night. What else can I do?" Does this sound familiar? God does know you are sick and he knows you want to be well and he knows you pray. This is all true. It's also true that we need to set about it his way. We need to follow God's plan and not our own. God longs for us to be perfectly whole, but will not force wholeness upon us. He provides the healing; he shows the way. We can take it or leave it. He provides skilled physicians. We can take them or leave them. He provides ordained ministers and other faithful believers to lay on hands and pray for people and to anoint the sick with oil. We can take them or leave them. God will not force his healing love and power upon us. It is our choice whether we want to reject or receive. We express this choice consciously and unconsciously, not only by yes or no, but by our response to God's requirements.

"You will find that doing the will of God leaves you no time for disputing his plans." Anonymous.

Obedience

Patricia, who was attending one of our evening spiritual journey courses, walked over to my wife after the class had ended. She asked her if she would pray for relief from her terrible migraines. This was now the third day that this particular migraine headache had persisted. My wife laid her hands on her head and asked God, in the name of Jesus Christ, to cause the migraine to go. With her thumb she made the sign of the cross on her forehead and stepped back. Almost immediately, Patricia appeared relaxed and peaceful and in a few seconds she began to smile. Then she opened her eyes and said, "I was very embarrassed and nervous to come and ask you to pray for me, especially in front of all these people. But I was praying by myself for this terrible migraine to stop and I heard God tell me to go over and ask you to pray for me. That was very hard for me, because I always have prided myself in not needing other people and never asking any one to do anything for me." Patricia heard God's will and obeyed even though initially her own personal will was in complete disagreement.

"Peace is the deliberate adjustment of my life to the will of God." Anonymous

It is God's will to make us whole

We believe emphatically that it is God's will to heal. Jesus Christ healed people in his earthly ministry. There are twenty-six specific instances recorded in the gospels where Jesus healed someone. There are also several references to him healing everyone in the town that he was visiting. He told his disciples to carry on his healing work. If it is not Christ's will to heal, why did he heal people? If it is not Christ's will to heal, why did he send out his disciples with specific instructions to heal. **"He, (Jesus), called his twelve disciples to him and gave them authority to drive out evil spirits and to heal every disease and sickness." (Matthew 10:1).** Here we have a mandate from Jesus Christ to carry on his healing ministry. There is not one incident in the Bible of Jesus telling someone that their sickness is the will of God and that they should suffer patiently with the understanding that their suffering would do them good. No, Jesus saw sickness as an enemy to be defeated and driven off, not something that you must grin and bear.

God's Rx:

Read God's Last Will and Testament, the Holy Bible.

Search the Scriptures for God's promises and instructions for your health and well-being.

Chapter Thirteen

▼

Bringing Our Picture of God into Focus

"More things are wrought by prayer than this world dreams of." Alfred, Lord Tennyson

Now that we know more about the will of our Father for our healing, we need to cleanse our minds of any and all false images that we have made of God. We must embrace with our minds, until we have it firmly established in our hearts, the truth that God is not, repeat not, the cause of our sickness, troubles, sorrows or death. He is the loving Father who sees these things as a tragic and malicious interference to his divine plan for our destiny. When we focus on him it is clear that he is the God of love.

Jesus said, "I am the resurrection and the life." (John 11:25). This is the word of God that speaks pleading to us across the centuries. Do not put on God's shoulders the blame for illness and sorrows that have been borne out of man's collusion with sin and the devil's malignant will for our destruction.

'Now wait a minute!' someone might say. 'Aren't we supposed to carry our cross? Isn't that what Jesus said?' Yes, he did indeed say that and yes, we are meant to carry our cross. But the context in which he spoke of carrying our cross has nothing to do with suffering through illness. Carrying our cross means having the courage to stand up for our faith and being willing to endure whatever hardships or persecution we may encounter for exercising freedom of speech and speaking up for the gospel message of Jesus Christ.

"God calls us to suffer for the gospel. He does not call you to sickness."
Receive your healing. Colin Urquhart

You may still be wondering about God's will. Could it be God's will that I am sick or, say, that my friend Jane lost her husband so young? Then, too, didn't Jesus himself pray to his Father, **"Not my will, but Thy will be done."**? When Jesus prayed this, it was at a specific instance, as Jesus prepared himself for the terrible suffering in the sacrifice that he was about to make, in taking on everyone's sins and infirmities on the cross. This was not a prayer for healing that he made. This was a prayer for guidance and direction. To make a comparison between our personal needs and Jesus contemplating his impending crucifixion is clearly misguided.

Whenever we are looking for the Lord's guidance and wisdom in decision-making it is always good to pray: "Not my will, but Thy will be done." But when we are praying for healing, if we say, "Please heal me, if it be Thy will," we are obviously suggesting that it may not be God's will to heal. This is clearly not a prayer of faith. Moreover, it is counterproductive to the state of mind of someone who is being prayed for, as it plants doubt instead of hope. This is not an accurate Christian teaching. It is just not consistent with the teachings of Scripture. There is a more faithful way that we can pray, saying: "Lord, may this healing take place, according to your perfect will."

"This is the confidence that we have in approaching God: that if we ask anything according to his will, he hears us. And if we know that he

hears us—whatever we ask—we know that we have what we asked of him." (1 John 5:14,15)

As you can see, where our idea of the image of God has been wrong, we must change it. This is not a trivial issue. It is a matter of life and death. He is not **a** god who wills suffering and death on his children. He is **the** God of Love. We all are his children, whom he loves, and he desires for us to return freely and voluntarily into a close and loving relationship with him.

Please God. Make an Intervention!

Many of us have cried out in our pain: "if you really are God and we really are your children, why don't you intervene?" But he has intervened! In fact, God ran the ultimate intervention. He has already intervened in the person of Jesus Christ to overcome our sickness, suffering, violence, jealousy, hatred, death and sin. "**For God so loved the world, that he gave his one and only Son, that whoever believes in him, shall not perish, but have everlasting life.**" (John 3:16). Even with this infinitely powerful, divine intervention, God still gives us the choice. He wants us, as Jesus himself clearly affirmed, to "**love the Lord your God with all your heart and all your soul and all your mind and all your strength.**" (Mark 12:30-32). But he does not twist our arm for that love. Only our uncoerced love and our willing obedience can satisfy God.

God's Rx:

Know that faith in God's healing power comes when we exercise it.
Put your faith into practice.
Your faith will require more action than belief.

CHAPTER FOURTEEN

▼

THANK YOU. THANK YOU. THANK YOU.

"Do not be anxious about anything, but in everything by prayer and petition, with thanksgiving, present your requests to God. And the peace of God which transcends all understanding will guard your hearts and your minds in Christ Jesus." (Philippians 4:6,7)

You might say that Paul, the writer of the letter to the Philippians, has got this backwards. Why on earth should I thank God for my healing, or the answer to any prayer, when I don't yet have the results? Isn't that being completely delusional? Why should I give thanks? Why? Because giving thanks in advance is a strong and positive expression of faith. Because we were created to be worshipful people, expressing love to our Creator, to the One who is the very source of love and the source of life.

"Praise God even when you don't understand what He is doing." Henry Jacobsen

God loves praise, as all the prophets and the apostles make absolutely clear, not because he needs to hear it, but because we need to give it. Thanking God through praise and worship is in itself a kind of prayer. It works in much the same way as prayer. It actually brings us more consciously into the presence of God. We are completely dependent on God for our existence. We are only able to take our next breath because God exists. Are we grateful? Are we ready to give him the honor and respect of thanksgiving and praise that is due him? Praising God is one way of showing our faith and our understanding that he loves us and he wants us whole.

Unable to give God the glory

A member of our church, Alan, came in early for the first Sunday morning service. He was visibly shaken, a fact that his customary cool, calm and collected composure could not conceal. With reluctance, he told us how the night before he had received a phone call from his son that completely stunned him. His son's girlfriend, who is a doctor, aged thirty-four, had just undergone some tests. Following an MRI and a biopsy she was diagnosed as having pancreatic cancer. In a small group we prayed for this young doctor. Alan thanked us for our prayers and he walked to a pew where he continued to kneel in prayer until the worship service began. Two Sundays later, we gathered in the back of the church to pray for healing. I asked if he had heard any news of his son's girlfriend and would he like us to pray for her? He replied, "No, that won't be necessary. She just had another MRI and biopsy. The first round of tests were inaccurate and it had obviously been a misdiagnosis. Apparently everything was fine and it was just a false alarm."

This scenario is a surprisingly common one. Was it a misdiagnosis or did God not in fact bring about healing between the two tests? Rather than thank God and tell people that a miracle has occurred it is easier for some people to say that the medical authorities had initially made a mistake. The first series of hi tech tests were wrong and the second were right and God had nothing to do with it! Wouldn't you imagine that this attitude must grieve God, that we bring him our prayers for healing in our time of need and then when we are doing better we dismiss him as having played absolutely no part in answering them?

"When it comes to life the critical thing is whether you take things for granted or take them with gratitude." G.K.Chesterton

Don't take blessings for granted

When we praise God and thank him regularly, we stop taking his blessings for granted. When we stop taking his blessings for granted and gratefully recognize him as the source of our blessings, we open ourselves up to receiving blessings from him in a way more wonderful than ever before. We should thank him for the gift of life itself. We should give thanks for God's love towards us and for God's forgiveness of our sins. Giving thanks and praise gets us in tune with God. It is essentially right to give God thanks and praise. Indeed it is the will of God for us to be thankful. We often find in Scripture that we are being encouraged to thank God.

"Give thanks to the Lord, for he is good; his love endures for ever." (1 Chronicles 16:34)

Giving thanks in advance—Perseverance pays off

"The will to persevere is often the difference between failure and success." David Sarnoff

Angela's brother and his family came to visit on vacation from Europe. She was very concerned about her six year old niece who was suffering from a chronic infection in her intestinal tract and who was constantly sick and often in pain. She brought her to a healing service and we all prayed for her. Her aunt, who had witnessed other people experience healing, was severely disappointed that there was no immediate improvement in the little girl's condition. She felt that God was not caring and questioned how God could let a beautiful little child suffer like that.

My wife and I counseled her that God was not to blame for the child's condition and that we should continue to pray regularly for her healing and at the same time give thanks to God for the healing that God was doing in the little girl. Angela argued and asked how could she possibly say a prayer of thanks when it was obvious that her niece was still quite ill. We explained to her that prayers of faith take place **before** there is any improvement and we encouraged her to offer prayers of thanksgiving, if for no other reason than as an experiment.

For more than a year the little girl was prayed for at the weekly healing services. Additionally her aunt was praying for her every day, giving thanks for the healing that God had begun in her. Then came the good news. She was free from any symptoms and free from pain. Her appetite had returned along with her energy. As you can imagine, a spiritual healing took place simultaneously in her aunt.

We are encouraged in the Bible to keep up this thankful and joyful attitude at all times. "**Be joyful always. Pray continually. Give thanks in all circumstances, for this is God's will for you in Christ Jesus.**" (1 **Thessalonians 5:16-18**). Give thanks in all circumstances, even including when things are not looking good. The difficulties we encounter do not have to dominate us and drive us into desperation. When the circumstances seem bad we can still be thankful. We can be thankful for blessings we have received throughout our life. We can be thankful for someone else's good fortune. We can be thankful for the hope of a better day. We can be thankful for life itself.

It seems we often take so much for granted, especially the small stuff. We might pray and give thanks for the bigger, more pressing issues. But we become easily disappointed when everything doesn't turn out the way we planned and prayed for it. The small stuff we often forget to give thanks for is probably not so small at all. Small stuff we neglected to be grateful for can look like this: You have plenty of food to eat. You have a friend. You have clothes to wear. You have a place to sleep. You have a car. It runs. You can read. You have a job. You have someone who prays for you. You have a church to belong to. You are alive. Thank you, God. Thank you. Thank you.

"Sing and make music in your hearts to the Lord, always giving thanks to God the Father for everything, in the name of the Lord Jesus." (Ephesians 5:19-20)

God's Rx:

Make a list of the 'small stuff' God does for you, day in, day out. Thank him from your heart. Get into the 'Thank God' habit.

▼

CHAPTER FIFTEEN

THANK YOU AGAIN. GRACIAS. MERCI. GRAZIE. DANKE.

"Thou who hast given so much to me, give me one more thing—a grateful heart." George Herbert

We need to give thanks for healing. We should thank our Lord for every improvement that happens, no matter how small or insignificant it may seem. If we cannot be grateful for small measures of improvement why would you imagine we would be grateful for larger measures of improvement? Of course, when we are sick we would like to get a hundred per cent better immediately. But if you feel just one per cent better, give thanks to God.

A man in his forties spoke to me about the constant pain in his legs. None of the doctors he had visited had been able to come up with a diagnosis for his condition. As a chef he was on his feet for hours on end and now he was unable to work because of the pain. I prayed for him and talked to him about being thankful for even a one per cent improvement.

The next time I saw him a few days later he said that he had felt one per-cent better the next day and another one per cent better the day after that. He was encouraged and said he was giving thanks for his improvement. Now he believed that there was hope for his complete recovery, one small step at a time. If you are in just a fraction less pain than before, tell God, "thank you." If someone tells you, "you look better," even if you don't feel better, thank God.

"If you actually look like your passport photo you aren't well enough to travel!" Sir Vivian Fuchs

We all know from our own life experiences how easy it is to develop habits that are unhealthy. Fortunately, with a little regular practice we can instead develop habits that are positively healthy. So let's start getting into the healthy 'Thank you God' habit.

"The major theme of my talks with patients is: Don't deny the diagnosis, just defy the verdict that is supposed to go with it." Head First. Norman Cousins

Attitude of gratitude

Having a positive attitude is generally acknowledged as being a good and healthy thing. There is no better way of developing and maintaining a genuinely positive attitude than by expressing gratitude to God. In fact, you cannot have a truly positive attitude to life unless you have a positive attitude to God. Anything else is just hype. An attitude of gratitude is free. A grateful person is a pleasure to be around. Gratitude in a person is beau-tiful to encounter. Gratitude will make you feel better. What a wonderful side effect. Quite simply, giving thanks to God is good for you.

I love to tell the story

"The mouth talks about the things that fill the heart." Matthew 12:34 (WMS)

Many of us can recount the history of our illness. We remember only too well and can tell the sad story of the deterioration of our health. We can tell a tragic tale of progressively worsening sickness and deterioration. It should be a cause for self-reproach that we cannot equally well recount the story of our improvement or regeneration. We so quickly take improved health for granted. Either that, or we complain that we are not really that much better. We need to be grateful for small improvements. If God sees that we take small improvements for granted we are clearly not appreciating him for his goodness and so we lose our connection to him. He wants to use our healing as a chance to restore not only our health but also our loving relationship with him. Positive reports and giving thanks are occasions for celebration that bring a satisfying sense of completion to the healing that the Lord provided. Telling the story of our improvement, however small, shows other people God's love and power and is a great encouragement for everyone who listens to these exciting reports.

In the words of that oldie but goodie song: "accentuate the positive and eliminate the negative." We must focus on the positive, actively looking for things to give thanks for. If you don't acknowledge a miracle, however small, you limit the likelihood of your being open to further and greater miracles. In giving thanks to God we open ourselves up to the possibility of seeing God work greater miracles in our lives. We strongly encourage people to come back to healing services or conferences or church to tell their miraculous story of how God has healed them.

Thanksgiving

It was a healing service in the middle of the week. There were only ten people there as we were about to begin. Then an elderly couple walked in. The woman was obviously in a great deal of discomfort and walked using a walker and with her husband helping her with each painful step. They came up and sat near the front. When it came to the point in the service where we asked for anyone who needed prayer to come forward to the altar rail, they came up. He was the first person in the row and when I asked him what he would like prayer for, he began to weep. With tears streaming down his face and his voice choked with emotion, he said that he was here for his wife Dorothy, and that he only wanted prayer for her. Her doctor had told her that she could only expect to live another six weeks. The cancer was in her lungs and her liver and had also metastasized to the bones. He told us how much he loved her and that he couldn't bear to be parted from her. We prayed for her. As Khara and I laid hands on her, we asked the Lord God to effect a miracle of healing in her. We told her that only God knows the time and the hour when we will die and that nobody else has the right to state how long you have left to live. She also asked for healing for her husband, who was much more distraught than she was at the prospect of her dying soon. We laid hands on him too and asked that God fill him with peace and hope and that he give him the strength to endure through all this. Then my wife asked him to hold out his hands and we anointed them with oil, with the prayer that every time he touched her, God's life-giving healing power would flow through his hands to her body.

After the service, as we helped them to their car, they told us that they were members of another local church and that a woman in their Bible study had urged her to come to one of our healing services for prayer and anointing with oil. We told her we would pray for her regularly and put her on the prayer list. We invited them to come back to the healing service next week and said goodbye. As the weeks passed we did not see them again. We wondered why they didn't feel the need to come back for more prayer, or someone said, perhaps she had died.

Almost a year went by and we were getting ready for the weekly healing service. In walked this elderly couple, only they looked much younger than before. At first, for an instant neither of us recognized her as she walked down the aisle. Conspicuously absent was the walker. She did not even have a cane. There was also a marked change in the form of a big smile lighting up her husband's face. As is our custom in our healing services, we asked if anyone would like to share with the group any healing that God has done in their life. Dorothy leaped to her feet and walked energetically to the front of the church. She bounced from one foot to the other and she waved her arms excitedly as she spoke.

When she had got up that morning, she heard God tell her that she needed to go back to the church where he had given her his healing touch and to publicly thank him and tell her story to everyone there. Tears started to run down her face, but they didn't prevent her from talking enthusiastically. She told us that her bone cancer was in complete remission and that the tumors in her lung and liver had shrunk away. The doctor said he was astounded at her recovery and that it defied explanation. She said her husband told the doctor that he knew that it was God who had healed her. The doctor had replied that there was no other possible explanation and that it had to be a miracle.

She then told us that she couldn't stop thinking about the story of the ten lepers and how it applied to her and she proceeded to tell us the story: One day Jesus went into a village and ten men who all had leprosy met him. They called out to him and asked him to have mercy on them and heal them. Jesus instructed them to go to the temple and show themselves to the priest. All of them were healed right there on the road. One of them, when he realized he was healed, came back, praising God. When he found Jesus again, he threw himself at his feet and thanked him. Jesus knew that the other nine were also completely healed of leprosy and expressed his disappointment that only one man out of ten took the trouble to come back and thank him and praise God. (You can read this story in Luke 17:11-19). Having told us the story, she said that she had come back to thank God publicly and to thank us for praying for her nearly a year before. Her coming back to express thanks and to share her story with us and let us see the evident good health that she was enjoying was a great encouragement to our small group of people who had been meeting every week to pray.

God's Rx:

Listen to stories of healing from other people.
Tell your story of healing to anyone who is willing to listen to you.

*　　　　　　*　　　　　　*

Developing an attitude of expectation-Healing is a process

"Do not be anxious about anything, but in everything by prayer and petition, with thanksgiving, present your requests to God." (Philippians 4:6)

We cannot stress this key spiritual truth enough. Healing begins in our spirit. Sickness, whatever else may be a cause, has spiritual malaise at its root. This spiritual malaise is the result of our separation from God. Healing comes from the Spirit of God and enters our individual spirit. It is a process. The healing moves from the spirit into the psyche and into our body. It may take time to manifest any physical signs of improvement. In which case it will also take patience.

"Have faith in God, Jesus answered. I tell you the truth, if anyone says to this mountain, 'Go throw yourself into the sea,' and does not doubt in his heart but believes that what he says will happen, it will be done for him. Therefore I tell you, whatever you ask for in prayer, believe that you have received it, and it will be yours." (Mark 11:22-24)

Ask God in all sincerity and faith for healing and give thanks for that healing. Yes, even before it happens! It may not make sense to say you are completely healed when you still have the symptoms, but it does make sense to say you are **being** healed, before your symptoms have improved. We don't need to wait to feel better or to notice improvements, or to get encouraging test results before we begin thanking God. We should start right now. "I thank you, Lord God, for your healing power at work within me. Thank you, Lord Jesus Christ for the healing that you have begun. I thank you heavenly Father, and I look forward to the changes that your healing power will bring in my body. I thank you that you have blessed my spirit with your Holy Spirit and that you are healing me."

God's Rx:

Commit yourself to an attitude of gratitude.

Decide to become a truly grateful person.

Thank God for what you have already received and for what you have yet to receive.

Expect miracles.

▼

CHAPTER SIXTEEN

OUR TOOL CHEST-TOOLS FOR HEALING

The term 'tools for healing' is not to suggest in any way that divine healing is mechanistic. However, there are certain things which we can do with our God-given abilities that will increase the likelihood of us, or someone we are praying for, receiving God's healing. So if we really want to be healed, or to be agents of God's healing for others, it makes sense to make the best use of these tools.

What's love got to do with it?

"Love cures people—both the ones who give it and the ones who receive it." Dr. Karl Menninger

When asked by a teacher of the law, which of all commandments is the most important, Jesus answered: "**The most important one is this...Love the Lord your God with all your heart and with all your soul and with all your mind and with all your strength. The second is this: Love your neighbor as yourself. There is no commandment greater than these.**" (Mark 12:28-31)

God loves you

Have you ever noticed that some of the strangest stories you read and some of the strangest movies you see are true stories? It has often been remarked that 'truth is stranger than fiction'. It is a strange but true fact of human life that people find it hard to believe that God really loves them. We ask ourselves the seemingly logical question, 'how could the Almighty God of Heaven and Earth really love me?' The problem with this line of questioning is that we are assuming that God thinks as we do. We may find all sorts of reasons why we are not lovable. But God does not think the way we do.

God has declared: **"For my thoughts are not your thoughts, neither are your ways my ways." (Isaiah 55:8).** God doesn't love us because we are lovable. God loves us because God is loving. Whether we are lovable or not is completely beside the point. **"We love because he first loved us." (1 John 4:19).** Yes, amazing though it may seem, God loves us just as we are. What's more he loves us too much to let us stay as we are. He wants us to be free of all that is oppressive, hurtful or sinful.

"Love occupies a majestic place in healing." Prayer is good medicine. Larry Dossey. M.D.

What it comes down to for each of us is the necessity of an absolute surrender in love to God in heart, mind, body and soul, because we love him. Even if it may seem difficult to make this kind of self-surrender, it's really essential to start making small steps in this direction. Start to surrender to God's love until it becomes ingrained into your nature. God's Word tells us that we are precious in his sight and that he loves us. We need to remember this and direct our love back to God.

"No eye has seen, no ear has heard, no mind has conceived what God has prepared for those who love him, but God has revealed it to us by his Spirit." (1 Corinthians 2:9,10)

"The key to all forms of the ministry of healing lies in our firm belief and total conviction that healing is part of the ordinary will of a totally loving Father." His healing Touch. Monsignor Michael Buckley

Is love God's cure-all?

In every healing there is a manifestation of both love and power. People can intuitively discern spiritual love. This is especially important for emotional or psychological healing. The value of knowing you are loved cannot be underestimated. So we need to let God's love be manifested to others through us. People can be so wounded by experiences of rejection, mistreatment or abandonment, that they find it hard to believe that God can love them. God's love flowing through us goes that extra mile. Mother Teresa, who exemplified compassion and caring to the world, said: "**The greatest disease in the West today is not TB or leprosy. It is being unwanted, unloved and uncared for. We can cure physical diseases with medicine, but the only cure for loneliness, despair and hopelessness is love. Where do we find that elusive healing balm? God is love. We are his children.**" A simple path. Mother Teresa

God's love befriends those who might have been treated unkindly by others, or who have been made to feel unworthy or unlovable. Love doesn't seek to be rewarded. It does not belittle people, or put them down, or condemn them. It is caring, compassionate and courteous. The love of God flowing through each of us meets other people's need for love. God wants us to manifest his love to one another.

"**It is when I am willing to love the people around me that I am also able to see that they will come out into that love to find healing.**" Good Lord deliver us! Rev. Al Durrance

Love is a verb. Act on it!

On several occasions when Jesus healed someone the Bible tells us that he saw them and had compassion on them. The love of Christ is real and great. It is not just sentiment. It is not patronizing. It is abundant and infinite. It is available to share with others. Much of the hunger for love every person feels, is really a hunger for God. For he is our Creator and it has been said that there is a God-shaped hole in each of our hearts. God wants to fill our hearts with his love and wants us, in turn, to share it with others. Look around at your wounded family or friends. Start there. Put your fear of rejection in God's hands and give your healing love to family, neighbors or coworkers. Jesus said: "**I tell you the truth, whatever you did for one of the least of these brothers of mine you did for me.**" (Matthew **25:40**). Love is an action word. It doesn't have meaning unless it is shared, so, what are we waiting for?

God's Rx:

Believe God loves you. Love God back. Recognize other people's need for love. Regularly ask God for a continuous refill of love so you can share it with other people.

CHAPTER SEVENTEEN

▼

"I GET BY WITH A LITTLE HELP FROM MY FRIENDS."

"My best friend is the one who brings out the best in me." Henry Ford

As well as seeking the healing touch of God, we need to seek the cooperation of our doctors, our family and friends, and don't forget our community of faith. A loving community of believers, trusting in God and his healing love, is a wonderful and potent tool for building each other's faith and expectancy. It is a very powerful force. Enlist your friends and family to pray for you. Ask them to keep a positive, faithful attitude and to help you to keep a positive, faithful attitude. We must not dwell on the negative aspects of our sickness.

"I need you to stand by me"

Many people do not experience healing simply because they are not able to withstand the weight of the doubt and unbelief of their family and friends. If they cannot stand in faith with you, ask them to stay on the sidelines and watch, preferably seen but not heard!

"Our mental beliefs and frame of mind are so influential in this matter of health that it follows that we ought to choose the attitudes that build up rather than break down our health." God wants you whole. Selwyn Hughes

Recruiting power teams

One day we received two messages on our answer machine from two members of our former church. They both left the same frantic message that a young lady from the church, called Deborah, had been hospitalized and was in critical condition. Would we please pray for her and get others praying for her. When we reached her family, later that day, we learned that this healthy young woman had suffered a massive stroke, while driving home from work. By the grace of God, she had pulled off the road for gas just a few seconds before the stroke hit her. She was in intensive care. She was paralyzed, unable to move, unable to breathe except with a respirator. The concern was that even if she did come out of the coma, there would be a very high probability of lasting brain damage. Her family were told that she would then almost certainly be in a vegetative state for the rest of her life.

We of course made a number of phone calls and enlisted a lot of people and churches to pray for her. Deborah's family and the people from her church contacted relatives and friends throughout the country and asked them to pray and to put her on the prayer list of their church. They called convents and monasteries in their area and asked them to include her in their prayers. Just how many people were included in this network of prayer is impossible to guess. After one month we received a report that she was out of the coma and no longer needed the respirator, but she was still paralyzed and was not expected to walk or talk again. After another month had passed we heard that she could recognize her family and that she could speak a little. The next few months were an extremely busy period for us and we did not hear any more progress reports.

Then we were invited to speak at a two day conference on healing at a location that was about one hundred miles from our old church. There were over two hundred people there, including twenty people who had come from our former church to see us and take part in the conference. What really caught our attention was to see Deborah walking in without any help. As is our custom, and as a faith building exercise at these kinds of events, we asked if anyone would like to share their healing story. We hoped that Deborah would take this opportunity, as we wanted to hear her share with all of us about her miraculous healing. After a couple of other people had spoken she gathered the confidence to stand up. Her voice was a bit shaky, whether as an effect of the stroke, or of the emotional impact of talking to so many people about what had happened, I did not know.

She said that one day, while driving, she heard a voice telling her to get off the freeway, a voice which she knew for certain was God's. She slowed down to pull over and said that was the last thing she remembered. Then later in the darkness of her coma that same strong voice reassured her that she was not going to die and that she would recover and be alright. Even as she came out of her coma, she could hear negative talk about her limited future possibilities, from people standing around her bed. At the same time she heard God's voice, telling her that she would walk and talk again. She said, "I trusted that voice and somehow I was never as worried for myself, as everyone else seemed to be." Now, she said, she had over ninety per cent of her faculties back. She had lost a considerable degree of memory. But she had resumed her old job and her employer and coworkers had helped to retrain her in her job-skills, which she was able to relearn reasonably swiftly. By then she was confident that much of her memory was returning and would continue to return. She was well on the way to again having a normal and fully productive life. What a wonderful answer to the prayers of many concerned and caring people. We give thanks to God and special thanks to her family and friends who mobilized a prayer army.

Seeking a healing community

We cannot over emphasize the importance of a 'healing community'. We have witnessed so many miracles in the settings of conferences and group meetings. There is a collective atmosphere of faith that gains strength in numbers. There is a communal spirit of love, acceptance and hopeful anticipation that occurs when people get together to look to the healing love of Christ. It is an environment that affords people the possibility of feeling secure enough to let go of the fear, or mistrust, or egotism which have kept them shut off from God's healing love. We really need to let go of those fears that isolate us from our fellow Christians. When we worship God together we become a community and we experience each other as a loving family. We are accepted. As we look around ourselves and see others in their fight against illness and we pray for their needs God helps us to forget about our own suffering. We can let go of our 'self,' as we bring the needs of others before God. Thus we make ourselves collectively much more open to God's healing love flowing through everyone who is present.

God's Rx:

Surround yourself with believing people who radiate hope.
Be honest about your need for prayer and for cooperation.
Commit with others to mutual encouragement.
Read books on healing miracles.

CHAPTER EIGHTEEN

▼

CALL ON YOUR FRIENDS IN HIGH PLACES—THE TRUE POWER TEAM

The Holy Trinity: God the Father and his Son Jesus Christ, who is the Great Physician and the Holy Spirit, who is the Great Comforter, are supreme. They are the source of all power in the healing ministry and in our personal fight against disease. There is no power in the universe greater than God's.

The Great Physician and his Assistant

As you read the stories in the New Testament about Jesus, you will notice that he is either healing someone, or he has just healed someone or he is on his way to healing someone. There are several references to Jesus going to a village and healing **all** the sick who were there. As you would imagine, Jesus encountered every kind of sickness, but the type of condition never prevented him from healing them all. He didn't walk in and say, "I'm really sorry. I can heal the migraines and the TB, but I don't do leprosy and I don't do cancer." No, he healed all of them. Jesus truly is the Great Physician.

God's prescription is the therapy of Jesus, the Great Physician. The original Greek word 'therapeuo' means to heal. It occurs thirty-seven times in the gospels, in reference to Jesus healing people. We generally think of the word 'therapy' in connection with physical therapy or psychotherapy. But we look to God for the ultimate healing of the whole person, body, mind and spirit. We are seeking the divine healing therapy offered by the Lord Jesus Christ. He said, "**I have come that they may have life and have it to the full.**" (John 10:10). He said "**I am the way, the truth and the life.**" (John 14:6)

John wrote about Jesus: "**The reason the Son of God appeared was to destroy the devil's work.**" (1 John 3:8) The word of God makes it quite clear what these works of the devil are, namely: sin, sickness, injustice, oppression, evil, disease and death. The Bible tells us that death will ultimately be destroyed by Christ, and that the power of death has already been conquered and disempowered by him.

God's Rx:

An important question we each need to have clearly answered in our own minds is: Are you willing to incorporate the Holy Trinity of God the Father, his son Jesus Christ the Great Physician and God the Holy Spirit who is the Comforter into your healing process?

Breaking the sin barrier with the sound of his name

"**The healing of the sick in His name is as much a part of the proclamation of the Kingdom as the preaching of the Good News of Jesus Christ.**" Lambeth Conference 1978—Resolution 8

Some people may initially feel uncomfortable saying the name of Jesus Christ in connection with their hopes of improved health. But the Bible tells us that there is power in invoking the name of Jesus Christ. His is "*the name above all names.*" His name releases the power of God's Spirit to expel disease and adverse conditions that are undermining our life force. His name is the key that opens the door to God's supernatural power.

"Therefore I tell you, whatever you ask for in prayer, believe that you have received it and it will be yours." Words of Jesus (Mark 11:24)

Jesus' followers, Peter and John, caused quite a stir among his opponents when they healed a paralyzed man. When questioned afterwards, Peter responded: **"If we are being called to account for an act of kindness shown to a cripple and are asked how he was healed, then know this, you and all the people of Israel: It is *by the name of Jesus Christ* of Nazareth, whom you crucified, but whom God raised from the dead, that this man stands before you healed." (Acts 4:9,10)**

We need to ask for healing in his name. In his name, we need to declare that sickness has no right to be in our bodies and that disease has no power over us. Through knowing him and calling on him, we can be set free from despair, distress, doubt and disease. Picture the living Jesus Christ in any distressing condition and call on his name. Remember that the name Jesus means: "He saves."

God's Rx:

Can we acknowledge Jesus Christ as our 'primary care' healer?

When you talk to God, ask for your healing miracle in the name of his Son Jesus Christ, the Great Physician.

*   *   *

The truth shall set you free

"I think the most important quality in a person concerned with religion is absolute devotion to truth." Albert Schweitzer

Jesus said, **"If you hold to my teaching, you are really my disciples. Then you will know the truth and the truth will set you free." (John 8:31,32)** One of his truths is that we can know the love, the healing presence and the unlimited power of God. Reinforce in your mind the truth of God's desire to see you healed. Jesus made a wonderful, encouraging and powerful statement, when he said, "**If you have faith…it will be done.**" (Matthew 21:21)

The not limited partnership

"**We can hold a correct view of truth only by daring to believe everything God has said about himself.**" A. W. Tozer

Jesus tells us repeatedly that through him we have authority and unlimited power. Behind everything we ask stand the words of the Lord Jesus Christ, "**it will be done.**" We are partners with Christ. This is not a limited partnership. Through Jesus Christ and the Holy Spirit, God gives us unlimited power. Being a victim of sickness and feeling powerless are not part of the deal. Jesus asks all of us to give him an opportunity to begin to manifest his power in our life, so that our healing will glorify his Father. He is vitally interested in your health, so pray to God the Father in the name of his Son, Jesus Christ.

God's Rx:

Read this often:

"**And whatever you do, whether in word or deed, do it all in the name of the Lord Jesus, giving thanks to God the Father through him.**" (Colossians 3:17)

Remember: "**By his wounds we are healed.**" (Isaiah 53:5)

*   *   *

Battle Plan—Waging war on sickness and disease

When you face a major challenge, whether it is your illness or a loved one's, the battle must be fought today. This is not the time to procrastinate. It is wise to have a battle plan. There is a well-known saying that if you fail to plan, you plan to fail. We don't undertake anything really important without a plan. We don't start a long trip across unfamiliar territory without a travel plan. Getting over your illness could be the fight of your life. Get your battle plan in your mind, in your heart and in God's hands. God's will is unconquerable. It knows no defeat.

Stand on Holy Ground, ready for Battle

Get the idea that through you, God is able to fight His enemies, evil and disease.

- Know that you are in God's will.
- Your will and God's will are allied against the enemy. They should be identical.
- You now 'will' this disease to leave. Your will becomes aligned with God's will; your command, his command.
- In the name of Jesus Christ, declare that this affliction has no right to take hold of this person.
- In the name of Jesus Christ, command the sickness to leave.
- The Trinity, the almighty supreme power in the universe, is guarding your back. See the battle won. Remember God's victory is complete.
- Push your way through every obstacle the enemy places in your way. Plant your feet on the firm and holy ground of every promise of God in the Bible.
- Don't give up before the enemy is conquered. God honors a persistent spirit.

God's Rx:

"Dear friends, if our hearts do not condemn us, we have confidence before God and receive from him anything we ask, because we obey his commands and do what pleases him. And this is his command: to believe in the name of his Son, Jesus Christ, and to love one another, as he has commanded us." (1 John 3:21-23)

*   *   *

The all important question—How big is your God?

Appoint Him the Real Commander-in-Chief

We need to ask ourselves this question. Do you believe that disease is more powerful than God? Does our God have unlimited love and unlimited power? If you say yes, he is all powerful, you must therefore believe that he is more powerful than your disease, stronger than your heart trouble, greater than your cancer. Christ's power to heal us is stronger than the power of disease to break us down. Remember Jesus regarded sickness and disease as our enemy, and so should we.

"Wherever Jesus meets sickness eating at a person's spirit or body, he regards it as his enemy and he cures it." Healing. Francis MacNutt

God's Rx:

Repeat to yourself over and again:
"Nothing is impossible with God." (Luke 1:37)

Keep your focus on winning the battle and you won't lose the war

"Go to sleep in peace. God is awake." Victor Hugo

A couple who attended church regularly, but were not in the habit of coming to other events, came one week to the Wednesday healing prayer service. As they came forward for prayer it was obvious that they were visibly shaken. James had just been diagnosed with prostate cancer and had been told that his prognosis was not at all good. He immediately became very concerned and depressed and resigned himself to a death sentence. We prayed for him. After two weeks he appeared to be in much better spirits. He had found a new doctor who gave him some hope and encouragement and had started him on a new experimental program of treatment. He faithfully followed his new program and zealously investigated every bit of information from the library or the Internet about this condition and its possible treatments. In his own way he became something of an expert on the subject. Soon he sounded like a cancer specialist. If you asked him how he was, he would respond by giving you his most recent white blood and P.S.A. counts. However his moods became dependent on his latest count. If the P.S.A. count was up, he was down. One Sunday his face looked ashen. Now the treatment was no longer working as he had hoped, and his PSA counts had risen to an all time high.

At the time for sharing communion, when he came up, I looked at him and felt the Holy Spirit prompt me to tell him to go to the back of the church, where someone would pray for him. It was our practice to have two people from the Healing Prayer group to be available at the back of the church, to pray for healing for anyone who wanted to be prayed for. But I had never before just instructed someone to go and be prayed for, feeling that people could take advantage of this opportunity if they wanted to. At the exact second that I was speaking quietly to him, I saw Khara get up and go to the back of the church. Later she told me that she just had this strong intuition from the Holy Spirit that she should go and pray for James and lay hands on him. As she put her hands on him she told him: "As I was praying for you a moment ago, I kept hearing in my head: "Tell him: 'Keep your eyes on the cross. I already carried your sin and your sickness. Keep your eyes on the cross, not on your P.S.A. levels.'" After the service Khara told me how much her hands had burned with intense heat.

When the next Wednesday healing service rolled around, James got up and shared with everyone present about what God had been doing in his life. He spoke of how I had told him very directly to go to the back of the church and how he found that he could not stop crying. He described how Khara had put her hands on him and that he experienced a charge of electricity that raced through his entire body, followed by the most intense heat. Four days later he could still fell the heat. He said he knew from that moment that he was in remission. Several years later he still is. He also takes an active role in a men's prostate cancer support group and is a leader in a vital men's ministry.

There is life transforming power

Sadly, in too many churches across the world each Sunday the wonderful, infinitely powerful news of God has been diluted down to mere good advice. Well meaning ministers tell us of Christian ideals and how we should conduct our lives. Then they send us out, under our own power, to try to achieve those high ideals. Left to our own devices, we are doomed to fail. Guilt quickly follows and often we move further away from God our Father at exactly the time we most need to be moving closer to him.

But the gospel message is not just good advice. God has given us the transforming power of Christ and his Holy Spirit, guaranteeing our rights as believers. We have only to believe that the power of Jesus Christ can and will make healing changes in our body, mind and spirit that we cannot accomplish by ourselves. With this belief firmly established in our minds we are moving well in the right direction.

God's Holy Spirit is the power at work in our bodies, our minds and our spirits. He can rid us of all negative feelings. Unforgiveness, resentment, anger, fear and depression can be dissolved by the power of God. God's healing power will make you whole and strong and set your mind free.

God is the Peacemaker

"God was reconciling the world to himself in Christ." (2 Corinthians 5:19)

'The world' means the people of the world. That means you. That means me. God is seeking a commitment from us. He wants us to make a choice to be reconciled to him and to live according to his ways. He wants us to have a day to day, living relationship with him. There can be no middle of the road, no half-hearted attempts. God is not satisfied with a lukewarm response from us. He wants our all. We need to surrender to God that which is due to him.

God's Rx:

God offers us the wisdom to use our minds in healing our bodies. Your imagination, when divinely directed, will penetrate through the physical body and the spiritual realm. Focus your attention, not on the pain and suffering, but on the work of healing that God has begun in you. Remember the battle has been won.

*   *   *

The Holy Spirit comforts the wounded

The gifts from God through his Holy Spirit are the holy weapons of God. God wants to dwell within us. God sent his Holy Spirit as our Comforter, so we can know the presence of the invisible, all-loving and almighty God within us. Through his Spirit, God's life-giving power penetrates each one of us and spreads into our heart, mind and body.

"The Holy Spirit writes his gospel in the hearts of the faithful" Jean-Pierre de Caussade

It is well known these days that advertising works primarily through giving suggestions to a person's subconscious mind, which then affects their choices and their actions. Think how much more the power of God, who created the human mind, can penetrate the subconscious mind through his Spirit. The very cells of our bodies can be penetrated by the Spirit of God bringing new life. The original Greek word for spirit in the Bible is 'pneuma,' from which we get the word 'pneumatic', and it means 'breath' or 'wind' or 'inspiration.' Inspiration—breathing in. To be filled with the Spirit means being supremely inspired. The Holy Spirit is also referred to as the "Comforter". We need to let the Holy Spirit of God work in us, to bring us real inner comfort, to inspire us, to heal us and to empower us to bring God's healing touch to others.

Spiritual Gifts from the Comforter

"The purpose of the gifts is to bring God's intervening love to particular situations." **Christian Healing. Mark Pearson**

There are a number of gifts of God's Spirit listed in the New Testament that we should be familiar with. St.Paul writes, "**Now about spiritual gifts, brothers, I do not want you to be ignorant.**" **(1 Corinthians 12:1).** Some of these spiritual gifts are particularly associated with healing. They are love, wisdom, knowledge, faith, healing, miracles and the gift of helping. When we integrate these gifts into our lives, we see changes occur in our spirit, our mind and our body. These changes are known as the fruit of the Spirit.

Who would not want more love? Who would not want more joy? Who would not want more peace, or more patience, more kindness, more goodness, more faithfulness, more gentleness and more self-control? These qualities are all available to us.

'**The fruit of the Spirit is love, joy, peace, patience, kindness, goodness, faithfulness, gentleness and self-control.**" **(Galatians 5:22-23).** These wonderful qualities develop increasingly in us as we make room for God's Spirit to fill us. We cannot experience these profound changes in our mental and emotional state, without also experiencing profound, positive and beneficial physical effects.

God's Rx:

Ask God to fill you with his Holy Spirit.
Ask him to develop his gifts in you.

                    *   *   *

The good doctor

The Lord created medicines from the earth and a sensible man will not despise them. And he gave skill to men that he might be glorified in his marvelous works. (Ecclesiasticus 38:4)

Now to more earthly matters. What is it that distinguishes the person we think of as a good doctor from the person who is not? Is it skill, training and experience? Certainly these are extremely important factors. But perhaps, underneath it all, the good doctor has God's gift for healing, whereas the other doctor merely has a job! We know it cannot be God's will for us to endure sickness, because he has given the art and science of medical healing to so many. Although it is true that medical science does not have the answer to every condition, the medical research and development that occurred in the twentieth century are nothing short of miraculous.

We need to acknowledge that medicine and scientific developments are, after all, gifts from God. Who, but God, gave people the wisdom and intelligence to learn, and the will to complete such extensive training? Who created the earth and the plants from which medications are formulated? God, in his grace, has given humanity the ability to develop in scientific discoveries and technological developments that have resulted in the cures of many diseases and have restored countless people to better health.

Will the doctor pray with you and for you?

We are not physicians and we make no medical claims or diagnoses, nor do we prescribe any medications. We do however make one suggestion. We suggest that you might want to consider finding a physician who is also a Christian. There is a directory you can write to in the back of this book that provides information about a network of physicians who are committed to Christian healing prayer. If you are facing serious medical problems and the prospect of surgery, would you not like to know that your doctor or surgeon is open to the guidance of the Holy Spirit in their diagnosis and treatment of you?

There is great comfort and support to be found through a doctor who is willing to pray for you and with you. As well as invoking the healing power of God, it also builds a greater sense of trust and partnership between you and your doctor. This also applies if you need inner healing and are seeking counseling or psychotherapy. You can trust that you will definitely be guided much better by someone who believes you are a child of God. Would you really want to place your psychological welfare under the influence of someone who thinks that you need to abandon 'childish beliefs' in a God who cares? Moreover, studies have shown that counselors who incorporate religious or spiritual approaches into their therapy sessions with their clients see much better results.

God's Rx:

Remember your part includes praying for your physicians, nurses and counselors.

CHAPTER NINETEEN

▼

THAT FAITH THING AGAIN!

"If we desire an increase of faith we must consent to its being tested."
A. W. Tozer.

"If you have faith as small as a mustard seed, you can say to this
mountain, 'Move from here to there' and it will move. Nothing will be
impossible or you." Matthew 17:20

What did Jesus mean when he told his followers that faith would make
them whole? Jesus was evidently pleased when he encountered vigorous
faith in a person. One day Jesus was asked to go to the house of a Roman
commander, a centurion, to heal his servant who was sick and dying.
While he was going to his house, some people met Jesus on the way, with
this message from the centurion. They said: **"Lord, don't trouble yourself,
for I do not deserve to have you come under my roof. That is why I did
not consider myself worthy to come to you. But say the Word and my
servant will be healed. For I myself am a man under authority, with
soldiers under me. I tell this one, 'Go,' and he goes; that one, 'Come,'
and he comes. I say to my servant 'Do this,' and he does it."** When Jesus

heard this, he was amazed at him. And turning to the crowd following him, he said, 'I tell you, I have not found such great faith even in Israel.' Then the men who had been sent returned to the house and found the servant well." (Luke 7:6-10)

There were other times when Jesus was obviously frustrated at the lack of faith that his followers exhibited. They who were with him day by day and saw him heal the sick and raise the dead and create food for thousands and turn water into wine, still had difficulty having faith. This doesn't immediately encourage us! You might wonder how we can be expected to have a faith powerful enough to effect healing for ourselves and for others.

God not only asks us to have faith, but he also gives us the potential to have faith. Faith is a free gift. All we need to do is ask our heavenly Father, in the name of Jesus Christ, to give us that gift. But there is a catch. Having asked for it, like the Roman centurion in the story above, we must exercise it. We need to put into practice a genuine and positively expectant faith in God's promise. He has shown us the way to faith and he has told us how to develop it. That way is with expectation.

Faith is strengthened by hearing the word of God. One of the helpful things that we can do to develop the gift of faith is to discover what God has done and what he has promised. As we read the accounts, recorded in the gospels, of healings that Jesus did, we learn more about the nature of faith. In some of the accounts of healing, such as the healing of the blind man, (see Matthew 9:27-31), we learn that faith was central to the healing. On some other occasions, such as healing the man at the pool at Bethesda (see John 5:1-9), faith wasn't particularly emphasized. Nevertheless, the very least that is required of us is an openness to the possibility that Jesus Christ can bring us healing. As Jesus himself said: "**Everything is possible for him who believes.**" (Mark 9:23)

How do we get faith?

It's almost too simple!

We get faith by asking God for the gift of faith. How do we develop that gift of faith? We develop it through a prayerful and systematic study of God's message, paying particular attention to the healing miracles of the Lord and his followers. There is of course a need for patience when believing God for a miracle, while apparently experiencing no improvement at all. Trying to sustain our faith can be difficult, but faith, by definition, is focusing on the evidence of things that are not yet seen. **"Now faith is being sure of what we hope for and certain of what we do not see."** (**Hebrews 11:1**). First you must keep believing and thanking God, before the healing is manifested. It takes no faith to believe in a healing **after** it has occurred and the symptoms have gone. Real faith comes into play **before** there is any sign of the healing having occurred.

Faith is continuing to run the race, assured that you will get your second wind. William Ward

Obviously the greater the faith of the receiver the better. However it is not faith in faith that heals. It is Jesus Christ who heals. Faith is only possible when we become sure in ourselves that Jesus is the Son of Almighty God, who came to rescue us from a destiny of misery, disease and death. When we are sure who he is, we begin to realize how relatively little our condition is, and how easy it is for him to heal. We start to gain confidence in a new perspective and realize that he can heal, he does heal and he wants to heal.

Faith means that we believe that God has the power to heal. Faith is confidence in the absolute love and power of God. It is also confidence in our ability to recognize his presence and our willingness to connect with his healing power. Our faith means that we acknowledge God is already at work. So we put aside our thoughts of anxiety and consciously develop an attitude where we expect a victory over our illness. We need to see that victory in our mind's eye and express our faith in prayer, in thanksgiving and in action. If you have placed your faith in Jesus Christ, God's Son, you have picked the winner, for he has won the battle between life and death. The victory is his.

God's Rx: Faith Steps

1. Ask God for the gift of faith.
2. Put faith into practice.
3. Study God's Word.
4. Obey His teaching.
5. Pass faith on to someone else. It is contagious.

CHAPTER TWENTY

▼

MEDITATION

"The object of prayers and meditation is always the same. It is to improve our conscious contact with God, with his wisdom, with his love and with his will." Keith Miller

"I will meditate on your precepts and consider your ways." (Psalm 119:15)

How many of us really take time out in our daily lives for our prayers, much less for meditation? But that sort of quality time is extremely important for us in our relationship with God. God asks us to be still and quiet and meditate. "Be still and know that I am God." (Psalm 46:10)

Why be quiet? Why be still? Because it is a way for us to come into increasingly close contact with God and to experience his presence. It is an opportunity for us to know him more personally and to have intimate communion with him. It is a chance for us to have a fuller, more heartfelt understanding of his teachings.

The secret is out

"In silence man can most readily maintain his integrity." Meister Eckhart.

There is a secret that Christians throughout the ages have known. It's called silence. A quiet time with God refreshes and restores our soul, our mind and our body. In our quiet time with him we find peace. Mother Teresa said that, "**God is the friend of silence. I begin my prayers in silence, for it is in the silence of the heart that God speaks.**"

In our quiet time with God we find peace and a new freedom. In quiet time with him you will find an energy and power that brings you into personal wholeness. This silence with God will increase your inner strength, renewing you to face the challenges of life.

What to meditate on:

"**To seek God means first of all to let yourself be found by him.**" Rules for a new brother. The Brakkenstein Community, Holland

Gratitude

We can practice a meditation of gratitude. That is we can simply thank God for all his blessings, and name them as we think of them. "Thank you Lord for love." "Thank you Lord for family." "Thank you Lord for friends." "Thank you Lord for my healing." "Thank you Lord for a good mind." "Thank you Lord for education." "Thank you Lord for my doctors and nurses." "Thank you Lord for…"

Meditate on your miracle

All of us have a God-given imagination. The problem is that our imagination often goes places we would prefer it did not go. This is especially true with illnesses where it is easy for our imagination to picture the worst and cause us to spiral down into depression. An uncontrolled imagination can be a liability. However we have a wonderful alternative which is to consecrate our imagination. Our imagination is consecrated when we dedicate it to God and we start to train our imagination to see life as God wants us to see it, through the eyes of faith. A consecrated imagination is an extremely helpful and powerful ally in the healing process.

Spend a little time regularly visualizing yourself healed. See yourself as God intends you to be, whole in mind, body and spirit. Picture yourself well. See the Holy Spirit filling your body with his life-giving healing light. Meditate on God's holy angels ministering light and life and health to you.

Meditation is biblical

The best definition of Biblical meditation is "to read, mark, learn and inwardly digest the word of God." There is healing, life-giving power in God's words. As we reflect on God's word, the deeper meaning starts to saturate our consciousness. This reflection facilitates the living word of God to transfer from the written word on a page directly into our hearts and minds.

One variation on biblical meditation is to take a whole passage of scripture as your focus. Choose a passage that has struck a chord with you or a passage that addresses a concern of yours. A good example would be: **"Praise the Lord, O my soul, and forget not all his benefits—who forgives all your sins and heals all your diseases."** (Psalm 103: 2, 3). Read it and reflect on it. Read it again and reflect some more. Read the same passage two or three times a day for several days. Pray over it, asking God to send his Holy Spirit to give you insight into it. He will.

God's Rx:

Select a verse of Scripture that is particularly meaningful to you, especially a verse about healing. Come into the presence of God through stillness and quiet. Meditate on that verse. A couple of examples are:

"I am the Lord who heals you." (Exodus 15:26)

"By his wounds I am healed." (Isaiah 53:6)

(See the index of healing Scriptures at the back of the book)

▼

CHAPTER TWENTY-ONE

FROM GOD'S MOUTH TO YOUR EAR

"I want to know how God created the world. I am not interested in this or that phenomenon. I want to know his thoughts. The rest is details."
Albert Einstein

The Manual

A couple of years ago we bought a new SAAB. As with all new cars it came with a manual. Being a European car it came with a manual bound in genuine Moroccan leather with the company name embossed on the front. Inside the manual SAAB told us everything we needed to know about their product: when to get a checkup, how many miles before it needs any replacement parts and so on. Then all of a sudden there is a warning: "If you take this product for repairs by anyone other than a SAAB agent the warranty is void." Why? Because they made it. They know it. They know what it needs. They know how to fix it. The same is true with these unique bodies we live in. God created the human body. He also gave us a manual. For some of us it is even bound in genuine

Moroccan leather with letters embossed on the front. This manual, given to us by our manufacturer, provides us with the finest guidance in how to live, how to act and even how to think. How often do we check our manuals, and how often do we follow the instructions in them?

Do you know how many miles you can go with resentment in your tank before a breakdown? We could say that our Creator is best qualified to take proper care of his creation, since he knows every moving part and even the ones that don't move, or that move a little slower than they used to. This wonderful manual addresses everything that is necessary for wholeness of life here and knowledge of where we will go when we leave here. When we run to other sources for the information that our manufacturer has already provided for us we may lose our warranty! So let us look to our manufacturer, our Creator, and see where he leads us.

"So God created man in his own image." Genesis 1:27

The words of God are living, healing and powerful. His words have the extraordinary ability to bring new life. Jesus said: **"Man cannot live by bread alone, but by every word that comes from the mouth of God." (Matthew 4:4).** There is tremendous encouragement in God's word. God's word is alive and brings healing. We need to remind ourselves of God's words and share his message with others. The more we contemplate the word of God the more it becomes part of the fabric of our thinking and our outlook on life. The words of God need to live in our hearts and our minds. As we read and study the Bible the presence of God's thoughts becomes greater than the pressure of our doubts and fears. As this happens we become well established in his healing way. With God there is no such thing as incurable.

"My Word will not return to me empty, but will accomplish what I desire and achieve the purpose for which I sent it." (Isaiah 55:10-11)

Can you imagine a mother who had this much faith in the words of God? Her teenage son was brought into a North Carolina Hospital after a motorbike accident. Most of his bones were broken. He had extensive head injuries and a ruptured spleen. He was put on life support. The doctor told the mother that her son probably would not make it. The mother called her church and asked for friends to volunteer to come in and read the Bible to him. She resolved that as long as he could draw a breath he would hear God's Word. For two weeks someone was reading Scripture to him around the clock. He no longer needed the life support systems and he was taken off the critical list. In a few short weeks he was sent home. What a blessing that his mother insisted on keeping him surrounded with God's messages from Scripture.

You now know that we don't need to strain to have faith. We just need to look with faith to Jesus Christ the resurrected Son of God. It is really a matter of just being in the love of Christ and taking his words to heart.

"My son, pay attention to what I say; listen closely to my words. Do not let them out of your sight, keep them within your heart; for they are life to those who find them and health to a man's whole body. Above all else guard your heart, for it is the wellspring of life." (Proverbs 4:20-23)

From your mouth to God's ear

Most people are familiar with the term confession. Confession literally means to agree with God. There are two types of confession and we need to put them both into practice.

The first type of confession is repenting and releasing. This means telling God honestly about those things in our life that we know to be wrong. The more we learn what God's Word says and apply it into our lives the more the Holy Spirit will tell our conscience what we need to let go of. When we repent, we turn away from those things and ask God for his strength to release the hold they have on us.

The second type of confession is a positive declaration of God's teaching. You cannot look in opposite directions at the same time. We cannot afford to be in two minds about this. Being indecisive about whether we have any hope of recovery incapacitates and depresses us. We need to affirm positively to ourselves the truth of God's teaching and his promises and claim them as being our own truth. What we confess with our lips directly affects us. Expressing doubt and disbelief, except when specifically repenting of them and asking for their healing, perpetuates them. If we frequently complain about our suffering and constantly let people know how bad it is, we reinforce in our own minds a sense of being dominated by sickness. Our focus is then always on how bad the problem is. It may indeed be very bad. But dwelling on it only tends to magnify the discomfort and make things worse. Dwelling on our suffering can drag us down into depression.

"What poison is to food, self-pity is to life." Oliver G. Wilson

If, on the other hand, we dare to be positive and affirming, and speak of how God's healing power is at work in us, we reinforce a sense of hope in our minds. The more we express hope and faith the more real they become for us. Let's have our mouths say what God says about our sicknesses and our health.

Business consultants who provide training courses in 'Time Management Skills' often talk about the 80/20 rule. This rule states that if you do not plan how to use your time well, 80% of your time will be used up on the 20% of your job that is least important. By contrast a well-organized person will have this the right way round. They will use 80% of their time to deal with their most important tasks.

There is a parallel to the balance between this and what the Word of God says and what your symptoms say about your health. Keep 80% of your mental energy on God's encouraging teachings and 20% on monitoring your symptoms, not the other way round. If God's life-affirming words point you towards renewal of life and your prognosis points towards deterioration, which way do you want to focus most of your energy on?

We need to remember that we share in the benefit of Christ's resurrection, both in the future for our souls, and in the now for our experience of living. Through paying enough attention to God's teachings we can arrive at the same degree of inner assurance concerning both the healing of our bodies and the salvation of our souls.

"The Lord is faithful to his promises and loving toward all he has made." (Psalm 145:13)

Focus on God's teaching more than on your symptoms. Affirm to yourself: "I am being healed" and give thanks to God for his healing power at work in you. Give thanks to God for his healing power at work in someone you have been praying for. We need to focus on God and what he says. So we direct our attention to the outcome, which is healing and health. We don't deny the sickness, but we refuse to accept that disease has any right to be in your body. You can tell yourself, "By his wounds I am healed, and I am going to believe God, not my circumstances or my feelings or my fears." By focusing our attention on God's teaching we are focusing in the right direction.

Please understand that we are not, in any way, advocating being irresponsible about sickness. Pretending that there is nothing wrong with you doesn't make it go away. What we are saying is simply that our focus and our energy are best directed toward the healing promises of God, not fixated obsessively on our problems.

God's Promises

We should always remember the passage of Scripture which tells us that: "The one who is in you is greater than the one who is in the world." (1 John 4:4) This is a wonderful verse. It reminds us of the amazing truth that God sends his Spirit to live in all believers. And importantly, his Spirit is stronger than the power of evil and sickness that is in the world.

When Jesus went back to his home town, Nazareth, he did not work any miracles. The lack of faith of the people blocked the flow of God's healing power. That lack of faith was their refusal to acknowledge that Jesus is the Christ. Jesus tells us clearly that: "If you remain in me and my words remain in you, ask whatever you wish, and it will be given you." (John 15:7).

God's Rx:

Keep in mind that God's Word has the extraordinary power to impart new life. Healing requires taking God's word to heart.

▼

CHAPTER TWENTY-TWO

IS THERE A HEALER IN THE HOUSE?

"Whenever I minister in healing I see myself as the servant of the Father dispensing his healing love as he wills to who he wills." His Healing Touch. Monsignor Michael Buckley

You can turn on the TV, almost any day of the week, and find something on healing. Either there is a healing service on T.B.N. or C.B.N., or there is a medical doctor on a talk show who has rediscovered the power of prayer and written a best seller. Or perhaps there is an investigative journalist from tabloid TV, trying to expose a healing evangelist. Healers of every kind seem to be all over the place nowadays. You might find yourself wondering who should I go to? Who should I trust? What should I expect?

God has given a special gift to certain individuals. This is known as a gift of healing. A well known person in the last century who had that gift was Kathryn Kuhlman. Another well known person was Padre Pio. There are many others alive today, who are ministering effectively. You might wonder if you too have a gift for healing. How God distributes his gifts is up to him. If you feel that God is moving you to seek out someone with a special gift of healing, you can ask God in prayer for discernment and guidance about who to go to. After Khara had been diagnosed with a terminal illness, we prayed to God to be led to the right people for both spiritual healing and medical assistance. God answered our prayers in a miraculous way. We discovered in the process that God wanted us to develop a healing ministry and write a book about his healing love and power.

Reaching others with Christ's healing

We may all have some aptitude for healing, but not all in the same way or to the same degree. Whether you feel you have a gift for healing or not, anybody and everybody can and should pray for healing. As people called to the healing ministry, it is our duty to share our story, and to teach and write about God's miraculous ability to heal. Putting our beliefs into action we pray often for the sick. We lay hands on people and anoint them with oil. When we speak at conferences we share with others the miracles we have seen and experienced.

God asks all of us who are called to ministry to be worthy of the vocation. **"I urge you to live a life worthy of the calling you have received."** (**Ephesians 4:1**). For our talks with 'the Great Physician' we must be clean and pure of heart. **"If I regard iniquity in my heart the Lord will not hear me." (Psalm 66)**. Therefore, it's a good idea to begin our times with God by first confessing the impurity in our lives, and asking him to cleanse, renew and inspire us once more.

As our faith and devotion to God increases, God gives us more patience and a greater capacity to love others. We then bring a positive atmosphere into our healing prayers, into our touch and into our visits to sick and suffering people. We all need to pray for discernment and to listen carefully for the person's real needs. Do we inspire the people we pray for with hope and encouragement, or do our own doubts sometimes weigh them down?

There are times when we visit someone whose illness is extremely severe and we find that we feel pulled down into a weary, discouraged and dark place. We must remember we cannot rely on our own ability and strength to minister to people. God is the healer and we need to turn again to God and ask for his healing power and strength. We need to ask him to refresh and renew us and to lift up our faith as well as the faith of the person we are praying for.

"Our human compassion opens the door into the soul of the other person, but into this open door must walk the conquering Christ who alone can heal." Healing Gifts of the Spirit. Agnes Sanford.

Find out what's going on

The causes of illness are many and varied. We can of course pray effectively for anyone, without knowing the specifics of their illness. God certainly understands their condition better than we ever could. In fact, when we ask what someone needs prayer for, it really doesn't help to get a lengthy medical history! On the other hand, without attempting to 'play doctor' or get into diagnosing, we who pray for divine healing, for ourselves as well as for others, can still benefit from having some broad idea and understanding of what is going on.

We need to consider any and all possibilities. It might be that a person is suffering as a direct effect of an accident or infection. Prayers for healing of those specific parts of the body and their restoration to healthy function are clearly in order. It might be that a person is suffering from psychological or emotional abuse. Therefore, we need to pray for them to be comforted with the personal knowledge that they are truly loved by God. All of us need to sense and personally experience the love that comes from knowing God. Otherwise talk about God's love sounds empty. God's love plays an absolutely essential part in healing.

It might be that the problem relates to some wrongdoing or sin in a person's life, therefore repentance is a necessary foundation for the healing. It could be that a person has been involved in some occult activities. Therefore, prayer for deliverance from these spirits is a necessary foundation for healing. It could be that a person is suffering from a chemical imbalance, in which case prayer and medical supervision would need to work hand in hand.

In considering all of the possibilities, there may be a combination of several factors, and it is always best to ask God for guidance as to how to pray for or counsel someone. In any event, we should pray for inner healing and comfort, since there is scarcely a person alive who is not a member of the walking wounded, carrying emotional pain and scars. It cannot hurt, indeed it can only help to regularly, diligently examine our lives and search our hearts and confess any and all sin. Who would not benefit from becoming better informed about nutrition and making a sustained effort to improve their diet? We should be willing to pray for deliverance from negative spiritual conditions or demonic attack. After all, in the prayer that the Lord himself taught us, he told us to pray, **"deliver us from evil."**

Touching people with the love of God

"Sympathy is your pain in my heart." Halford Luccock
There is a wonderful thing that happens to any of us when we are touched with love. Conversely, it is a sad truth that children in institutions separated from human touch have a higher mortality rate. Why? It seems apparent that God's life-giving power is able to flow from one of his children to another. Jesus experienced that flow of power to another person. Once a woman tried to just touch Jesus's cloak, believing that if she could just touch his clothing she would be healed. When she did, Jesus immediately felt his healing power flowing out, and he asked, **"Who touched me? Someone touched me. I know that power has gone out from me."** (Luke 8:45,46).

Healing hands

Touching communicates love and concern. The benefit of touch is known by all caring people. The laying on of hands gives a person a sense of love and love heals.

"Healing is a part of our nature. We instinctively know this when we place our hands on a small animal or a little child in order to give peace and comfort." Healing gifts of the Spirit. Agnes Sanford

The healing touch may feel like a gentle warmth or like very intense heat. It might feel like a tingling, or at times even like an electric current. But what it feels like is not really important. What is important is that we touch the people we are praying for with the love of God. When you lay hands on someone with love and you pray for them, God can use your hands as the point of contact for the flow of his healing power into that person. If you feel called to minister to people in this way, offer your hands into God's service and ask him to consecrate them and to use them for healing.

"When we pray over someone, the Spirit will gently open us to the person who asks for healing, and there will be a union of spirits between us." His healing touch. Monsignor Michael Buckley

The gift that keeps on giving

There are a variety of healing related gifts such as comfort, encouragement, wisdom and knowledge. God has already made these gifts available to all of us who choose to follow him. We just need to recognize them. The list of gifts is impressive but they are always given by the same Spirit and the same Lord. Those of us who want to be used in the healing ministry of Jesus Christ need to offer ourselves humbly, as channels through which God's healing gifts can flow. There is an old saying, "the cleaner the pipes, the cleaner the water." The same can be said of working in Christ's healing ministry. For us to be more effective channels of God's love, grace and power, we need to cleanse and purify our hearts.

God's Rx:

Pray: "**Create in me a pure heart, O God, and renew a steadfast spirit within me.**" (**Psalm 51:10**) Offer yourself as an instrument of God's healing. Love people. Pray for people. Touch people with the love of God.

CHAPTER TWENTY-THREE

▼

IT'S TIME TO MEET THE GREAT PHYSICIAN

An attractive young woman in a bright white uniform with a pleasing smile looks intently at the young man sitting in the waiting room who appears lost in thought. She walks over to him and leans toward him. She gives him a comforting touch on his shoulder and awakens him from his reverie. "He will see you now," she says, her voice resonating with kindness and compassion. The young man nervously gets to his feet and follows her. He walks hesitantly over to the door. She opens the door, beckoning him to go on in. He enters a brightly lit, beautifully furnished room. His eyes move to the plaques on the wall and he nervously studies one as he waits for the man sitting behind the desk to look up from his book. He wonders to himself what the doctor is reading.

One of the plaques catches his eye and he reads:

"**Love the Lord your God with all your heart, with all your soul and with all your mind, and love your neighbor as yourself.**"

A strong yet gentle voice startles him from his preoccupation with the writing on the plaque.

"Can I help you young man?"

"Yes sir. Well I hope so."

Nodding his head towards the chair across from him, the physician says, "Have a seat." The kindness in his eyes and the caring in his voice put the young man at ease as he settles into the comfortable chair. As the physician puts aside the book his eyes focus on the young man. His eyes are at one and the same time penetrating and compassionate. The young man strains to see what the title of the book is, but he can't quite make it out. The deep resonance of the physician's voice makes him increasingly conscious of the direct but kindly gaze of the physician's eyes inviting him to speak openly. "Well, tell me about it," he says.

"You see sir, I have been to three other doctors and I've had every test you could imagine." His voice begins to crack. "They all say that I'm going to die."

The physician smiles at him and the smile is curiously comforting. "Son, everyone's going to die someday." He somehow makes this sobering truth sound agreeable.

"Yes I know that, but," choking back the tears, he says "but you don't understand. They said I only have a few months at the most. I'm too young to die!"

The physician, leaning forward across the desk and looking intently at the young man, said: "Hold on. Do you know that no one has the right to tell you when you are going to die? Now I have a question for you. How long do you think you might have?"

The young man feels agitated at this question. "I don't know sir, the tests show…" He starts to cry. Although he tries to stop himself, he sobs audibly and buries his face in his hands. Suddenly he hears himself saying, "Oh God, I'm so afraid. I feel like I haven't even started to live yet and now they tell me I'm going to die!"

The physician reaches over and with great compassion in his voice asks, "Son, what do you want from me?"

"Well sir, people say you can heal anyone," he pauses, hesitating. Then he lifts his face out of his hands and looks at the physician, "if you want to."

"If people have told you that, why haven't you got in touch with me before now?"

The young man lowers his head again, deliberately avoiding the physician's eyes. "Frankly sir, I trusted science alone to fix me and your way seemed a bit weird, you know, out of date, superstitious and sort of old-fashioned."

"Son, I could have worked with your doctors."

"I don't know if they would have accepted your approach."

"You'd be surprised at how many do. So it looks like I'm your last resort then, young man?"

"I guess so. Yes."

"You know, son. I hear from millions like you. I have to tell you it always makes me sad me that people only turn to me when all hope seems lost. Nonetheless, I am delighted to see you now."

The young man lowers his head to his hands and with tears flowing down his cheeks and through his fingers, he says, "I'm so sorry. Will you help me, please?"

The physician hands him a tissue. With striking authority in his voice he asks, "Do you really want to be healed?"

The young man looks up and winces, "How can you ask that?"

With that same conviction in his voice he replies, "It's a very important question."

The young man's eyes are now riveted on the physician's face. "Oh yes, more than anything. I really want to get well. I want to live!"

"Good. Now I'm going to give you a prescription," says the physician as he picks up his pen.

The young man protested, "But sir, you haven't made a diagnosis yet." He picks up the folder next to him and reaches to hand it to the doctor. "Don't you want to see my test results?"

The physician puts down his pen and looks the young man straight in the eye with a penetrating look. With resounding clarity in his voice he asked, "Son, do you believe I can heal you?"

The young man is startled. He stops for a moment to think. Then, suddenly finding a new sense of assurance bubbling up inside him, he looks directly back into the clear, loving eyes of the physician and says, "Yes sir. I do." Evidently pleased at the young man's response, the physician says, "Oh, I love to hear that."

The young man, greatly relieved, takes a deep breath and relaxes back in his chair. The physician hands him a piece of paper along with the book he had been reading earlier. "You need to do what I say, down to the last word."

"No problem, sir." A big grin spreads on his face as his hope is renewed.

"No, son you don't understand. I mean for the rest of your life here on earth." The young man seems a bit bewildered, but he hears himself saying. "All right, sir, I will." He glances down at the book in his hand. "But sir, this is a Bible. This isn't a prescription."

"Oh, but it is." replies the Physician with a radiant smile. The young man stands up and prepares to leave. As he reaches the door he turns around and says "Can I ask you just one more question? Are you really who I think you are? I mean are you really God, like the one who made heaven and earth, kind of God?"

Q & A

There are times when we or someone close to us needs to answer the following question.

The name of this game is "**Do you want to be healed?**"

Question: What is meant by the word terminal?

A. A bus stop   C. A deadly disease
B. A computer link   D. It's time to seek God

Answer: Hmm. C. No, wait. No, D.
Question: Is that your final answer?
Answer: Yes. D. That's my final answer.

APPENDIX

▼

Scripture references

Except where otherwise indicated Scripture Quotations are taken from:

The New International Version, (NIV) published by Zondervan. Other translations quoted are King James Version. (KJV); Revised Standard Version (RSV); Young & W.M.S.

Quotations from Ecclesiasticus are taken from The Revised Standard Version, including Apocrypha. Nelson.

Words to live by: Index of healing scriptures:

We invite you to continue your exploration of Christ's healing ministry and we encourage you to search passages from Scripture that relate to God's healing and his promises. Ask God to help you apply them to your healing and to the building of your faith. Taking the time and effort to learn what God has to teach you about healing will transform your life. You may want to study these Scriptures with a group of people who share your interest in the Christian healing ministry.

Love
John 14:15-25
Romans 8:28-31
Romans 13:8-10
1 Corinthians 13:1-13
Ephesians 4:2
Colossians 3:12-15
1 Peter 4:8
1 John 4:7-21
2 John 1:5-6

Faith
Isaiah 53:4-7
Matthew 8:5-13
Mark 10:46-52
John 14:11-14
Acts 3:16
Philippians 4:13
James 2:14
1 Peter 2:24

Anointing with oil
Mark 6:12-13
James 5:14-16

Name of Jesus
Acts 3:16
Acts 4:29-31
Acts 9:32-35
Romans 10:13
Philippians 2:1-11
James 5:14
1 John 3:23, 24
1 John 5:11-15

God's Word
Psalm 107:19-22
Proverbs 12:18
Proverbs 12:28
Proverbs 4:20-25
Proverbs 15:4
Matthew 4:1-11
Romans 10:17
2 Timothy 3:16-17

Promises of God
Exodus 15:26
Exodus 23:25
Psalm 91
Isaiah 54:10
Joel 2:28,29
John 5:24
John 6:35
John 6:40
John 11:25
John 14:2
John 15:26
1 John 5:14,15

Commands of God
Exodus 20:1-17
Matthew 6:14-15
Mark 12:29-30
John 13:34

Forgiveness or anger
Psalm 25:11
Psalm 51
Matthew 6:12-15

Mark 11:25
Luke 6:37
Ephesians 4:22-32
Colossians 3:12-15
1 Thessalonians 5:14-18

Prayer
Matthew 6:5-13
Matthew 19:13
Mark 11:22-25
Ephesians 6:18
1 Thessalonians 5:16-19
James 5:13-18
1 Peter 3:7
1 Peter 4:7

Healing touch
Acts 3:1-10
Acts 5:12-16
Acts 8:6,7
Acts 9:17-19
Acts 19:11,12
Acts 28:7-9
1 Corinthians 12:7-11
James 5:14-16

Obedience
Deuteronomy 30:11-20
Psalm 37:4-6
Psalm 84:11
Psalm 119:65-72
Proverbs 15:29
Romans 8:5-13
1 John 3:21-24,

Temple of The Spirit
1 Corinthians 6:9-20
2 Corinthians 6:14-7:1

Compassion
Matthew 14:13,14
Matthew 20:29-34
Colossians 3:12-15
James 5:11

Holy Spirit
John 14:15-18
John 16:13-15
1 John 3:24
Acts 1:4-8
Acts 2:1-24
Acts 10:44-48
Romans 8:1-39
1 Corinthians 2:6-16
1 Corinthians 12:1-11
2 Corinthians 13:14
Galatians 4:6,7
Ephesians 1:13,14
Ephesians 5:18
1 Thessalonians 1:4-6

Anxiety, Fear
Psalm 46
Matthew 6:25-34
Romans 8:15
Philippians 4:6,7
1 John 4:15-19

Peace of God
Proverbs 14:30
Proverbs 17:1
Isaiah 53:5
John 14:27
2 Corinthians 13:11
Ephesians 2:14-17
Philippians 4:7
1 Thessalonians 5:12-13

Choice
Deuteronomy 30:19,20
Joshua 24:14-18

Angels
Psalm 91:9-11
Hebrews 1:14
Hebrews 13: 2

Cooperation
Romans 12:9-21
Romans 13:8-10
Romans 14:7-10
Romans 15:5-7
1 John 3:11-18

Beware of the devil
Ephesians 4:25-32
2 Timothy 2:22-26
Hebrews 2:13-15
1 Peter 5:6-11
1 John 3:7-10

Wisdom
Romans 8:5-16
1 Corinthians 3:18-20
Ephesians 4:23,24
Ephesians 5:15
Philippians 4:8,9
Colossians 1:9-14
James 3:13-18

Strength
Isaiah 40:31
Philippians 4:13
Nehemiah 8:10,11

Blessing
Numbers 6:24-27
Proverbs 29:18
Malachi 3:8-12
Matthew 5:3-11
1 Thessalonians 5:23-24
Revelation 1:1-3

Grace
2 Corinthians 12:9
Ephesians 2:4-9

Thanks and praise
1 Chronicles 16:8-12
1 Chronicles 16:34
Psalm 92
Psalm 95:1-7
Psalm 96
Psalm 98
Psalm 100

Psalm 103
Psalm 105:1-15
Psalm 138
Luke 17:11-19
Acts 3:6-10
Ephesians 5:4
Ephesians 5:15-20
Philippians 4:6,7
1 Thessalonians 5:16-19

Joy
Proverbs 12:25
Proverbs 14:30
Proverbs 15:13
Proverbs 15:30
Proverbs 17:22
Philippians 4:4-7

Encouragement
Romans 12:4-8
1 Thessalonians 5:11
Hebrews 3:12-14

Serving God
Exodus 23:25
Matthew 4:8-11

Healing Miracles of Jesus
Matthew 8:2-4
Matthew 8:5-13
Matthew 8:14-15
Matthew 8:28-34
Matthew 9:2-7
Matthew 9:18-19, 23-25

Matthew 9:20-22
Matthew 9:27-31
Matthew 9:32-33
Matthew 12:10-13
Matthew 12:22
Matthew 15:21-28
Matthew 17:14-18
Matthew 20:29-34
Mark 1:23-36
Mark 1:30-31
Mark 1:40-42
Mark 2:3-12
Mark 3:1-5
Mark 5:1-15
Mark 5:22-24, 38-42
Mark 5:25-29
Mark 7:24-30
Mark 7:31-37
Mark 8:22-26
Mark 9:17-29
Mark 10:46-52
Luke 4:33-35
Luke 4:38-40
Luke 5:12-13
Luke 5:18-25
Luke 6:6-10
Luke 7:1-10
Luke 7:11-15
Luke 8:27-35
Luke 8:41-42, 49-56
Luke 8:43-48
Luke 9:38-43

Luke 11:14
Luke 13:11-13
Luke 14:1-4
Luke 17:11-19
Luke 18:35-43
Luke 22:50-51
John 4:46-54
John 5:1-9
John 9:1-7
John 11:1-44

Healing Miracles of the Apostles
Acts 3:6-9
Acts 5:12-16
Acts 9:17-18
Acts 9:33-35
Acts 9:36-41
Acts 14:8-10
Acts 16:16-18
Acts 20:9-10
Acts 28:3-5
Acts 28:7-9

BIBLIOGRAPHY AND SUGGESTED FURTHER READING

▼

Augsburger, David. *The freedom of forgiveness.* Moody

Beckmen, Richard J. *Praying for wholeness and healing.* Augsburg

Bosworth, F.F. *Christ the Healer.* Power Books. Revell

Buckley, Michael. *His Healing Touch.* Fount

Carey, George. *I believe.* SPCK.

Cousins, Norman. *Head First.* Penguin.

Dossey, Larry. M.D. *Prayer is good medicine.* Harper Collins

Durrance, Al. *Good Lord Deliver us.* Wilmington Printing

Gardiner Neal, Emily. *Celebration of healing.* Cowley

Graham, Billy. *Peace with God.* Grason

Hughes, Selwyn. *God wants you whole.* Kingsway

Kenyon, E.W. *The wonderful name of Jesus.* Kenyon Gospel Society

Kenyon, E.W. *Jesus the Healer.* Kenyon Gospel Society

Larson, Drs. David B.,& Susan. *The Forgotten Factor in Physical and Mental Health:*
What does the research show? National Institute for Healthcare Research.

Lewis, C.S. *Miracles.* Touchstone. Simon & Schuster

Lewis, C.S. *Mere Christianity.* Macmillan

MacNutt, Francis. *Healing.* Ave Maria Press

MacNutt, Francis. *The power to heal.* Ave Maria Press

Miller, Keith. *A hunger for healing.* Harper Collins

Mother Teresa, *A simple Path* Ballantine

Murray, Andrew. *Divine Healing.* Christian Literature Crusade

Pearson, Mark. *Christian Healing.* Chosen Books.

Reed, William Standish MD. *Surgery of the Soul.* Christian Medical
    Foundation.

Sanford, Agnes. *Healing Gifts of the Spirit.* Harper & Row

Sarno, John E. M.D *Healing Back Pain* Warner

Tournier, Dr. Paul *The whole person in a broken world.* Harper & Row

Tozer, A.W. *Faith beyond reason.* Christian publications.

Urquhart, Colin. *Receive your healing*

Weil, Andrew. M.D. *Spontaneous Healing.* Ballantine.

Womble, Rufus J. *Wilt thou be made whole?* Democrat Printing

Recommended Resources:

▼

Healing Conferences

The authors Reverend Hugh and Khara Bromiley regularly speak at healing conferences. To inquire about such conferences you may contact: email: *FrBromiley@aol.com* or call 912-786-0881

Audiotapes of Healing Scriptures read by Reverend Hugh Bromiley may be ordered.

Email: *FrBromiley@aol.com* or call 912-786-0881

The Order of St.Luke

The International Order of St.Luke the Physician is an organization whose members are committed to the spread of Christian Healing. Local chapters of the OSL exist around the United States and in Canada, Australia, the Bahamas and the United Kingdom. OSL puts on healing conferences all over North America and internationally. The Order of St.Luke also publishes a monthly journal of Christian Healing, called Sharing.

The Order of St.Luke. P.O.Box 13701. San Antonio TX 78213 (210-492-5222). Website: *www.orderofstluke.org*

The Christian Medical Foundation, International Inc. is an association of medical practitioners who believe in Christian Healing. Founder: Dr. William Standish Reed

P.O.Box 152136, Tampa FL 33684. (813-932-3688)